MEETING THE WRITER'S DEADLINE

Finishing Your Book On Time And On Budget

Tonya Price's Fiction

Short Story Collections

Fiction River: Hidden Crime

Strange New Worlds III

Strange New Worlds IV

Strange New Worlds V

Upcoming Short Stories in Fiction River Anthologies

Hard Choices Anthology – Thriller short story, "Pay Back"

Stolen Anthology – Mystery short story, "Stealing Amy"

Feel the Love Anthology – Romance short story

Spies! Anthology – Thriller short story

2017 fiction novel releases

Virgin Soldier – International Thriller

Dead *Wrong in Gorlitz Park* – International Thriller

Get Me To The World On Time – Science fiction/ paranormal romance

2017 Business Books For Writers Series

Completing The Writer's To-Do List

Pricing The Writer's Books

Meeting the Writer's Deadline

Finishing Your Book On Time And On Budget

Tonya D. Price

Magnolia Lane Press

Meeting the Writer's Deadline

Published by Magnolia Lane Press www.MagnoliaLanePress.com

A "Business Books for Writers" series book
www.BusinessBooksForWriters.com

ISBN: 978-1-68384-002-2

Copy Editor: Lyn Worthen, Camden Park Editing,
www.camdenparkediting.com

Cover Design: ZoranFiver, www.fiverr.com

Cover photo credit: istockphoto, www.istockphoto.com

Interior Design: Dean Fetzer, GunBoss Books, www.gunboss.com

Author photo credit: Morin Studio of Photography,
www.morinstudio.com

Contents

Introduction

Finishing your book by the designated deadline is so important for your professional reputation, that it is the subject of the second book in the *Business Books for Writers* series. If you struggle with deadlines, and find yourself often missing due dates for your book, blog, or article, this book will provide strategies, tips and aids in getting you on track to complete your book project on time.

Many writers find that while they have the goal of publishing books, they never finish their books. The key to achieving any goal is to set a deadline. Research studies have shown that if you commit to a deadline, announce the deadline and track your progress toward achieving that deadline you have a significant chance of hitting that deadline.[1]

How this book builds on The Writer's Business Plan

The first book in the Business Books For Writers series demonstrated how to create a business plan with specific goals so you could build on your success throughout your career.

Now you need to *execute* your plan, and that means you need to write books on a regular basis, year after year. You can't succeed in this business if you don't set deadlines for your goals or if you consistently miss those deadlines.

If you have a co-author, you need to hit your agreed-upon deadlines, or they will lose interest and move your joint project to the bottom of their to-do list. They set their schedule based on when you will send them your part of the book. You can put your co-author in a difficult situation if you miss your deadlines. Also, they make commitments with their graphic artists, copy editors, and possibly other co-authors based on your project's deadline. If you miss your deadline, they may drop out altogether.

If you have sold a book to a traditional publisher, you have a deadline by which you need to deliver a final manuscript. If you are late, you will not endear yourself to your editor or the acquisitions department. However, if you meet your deadlines, book after book, your publisher will respect you and tend to buy more of your work.

It is very rare indeed that someone gets wealthy writing just one book! It can happen. It does happen, and I hope it happens to you but the typical path is that writers make their money by writing numerous books. The most successful self-publishers know that the more books they have for sale, the more money they make.

When readers find a book they love, they seek out more books by the same author. Many authors like to write within a series, using the same characters. Series books are quite common, and for good reason; readers enjoy going on multiple adventures with characters they like.

The more books you have readers to buy, the more money you make. Money you can put into marketing, better cover design, etc. In other words, the more money you will have available to get more people to buy your books, the more money you will have to produce audio books, book bundles, and other revenue streams. Increased revenue also creates the potential for offering discounts or free give always, and taking advantage of other marketing and advertising opportunities.

The key to *selling* more books starts with the goal of *writing* more books and finishing by designated deadlines. This includes all the tasks that go into producing and selling your books. Cultivating the ability to meet deadlines is one of the greatest assets any professional can possess.

So let's get started!

Checklists and example sheets

Tracking your writing is easier if you have the right tools. Business Books For Writers has provided a number of checklists and sample aids on their website to help you keep your book project running smoothly.

Website resources for this book

New tools are constantly being released to help professionals meet their deadlines. To keep you up to date we have provided a resource page for this book on the

Business Books For Writer's website. You can find the information at

www.BusinessBooksForWriters.com/Resources

Want easy access to the online links while reading? Go to

www.BusinessBooksForWriters.com/mtwd-links

Tips, helpful hints and warning boxes

A number of readers wrote to say they liked the tip, "helpful hints and warning boxes" in *The Writer's Business Plan*, so they are included throughout this book as well. Below is your first Tip box!

TIP: Read for ideas, but use what works for you

This book identifies why deadlines are important and presents a number of ideas of how you can improve the process you use to write your books and to produce your books if you are an indie publisher.

The GOAL of this book is to help you develop a process to complete your book project by a deadline.

Try the ideas presented here on small projects – a blog post or a short story, even if you don't believe they will work for you. You might be surprised and find out these ideas work quite well! If so, expand them to a book project.

You will try some ideas that do not work for you. Great! Now you know more about your writing process. Don't be surprised if you find some value in these ideas. If so, experiment – retain those aspects of the ideas that do work for you.

Your GOAL while reading this book should be to develop a process that works for you. You may discover bad habits that are limiting your ability to meet a deadline. Work on eliminating those bad habits rather than rejecting the information.

In the process of researching and writing this book, I have had a number of writers tell me that just the thought of doing any organization or tracking of their time makes them nervous. You have to commit to wanting to pursue a writing business to benefit from this book. It is perfectly fine to write just to tell yourself or your family your stories. You don't need to worry about deadlines if that is your goal. If you want to make enough money to cover your writing bills and no more, then you can probably get away with not worrying about deadlines, but if you want to make enough money to live off your writing, if you want to be a professional writer, then learning how to consistently meet your deadlines is a requirement.

This book was written to help professional writers to be successful in meeting their deadlines. If you want to be a professional writer but are afraid the business side of writing will harm your creativity read M.L. and M.L. Buchman's book, *Managing Your Inner Artist/Writer: Strategies For Success.*[2]

Chapter 1: Overview Of A Book Project

Writing a book is a project

You have a book to write. Maybe you sold that book to a traditional publisher and they have given you a deadline for submitting the manuscript with requested revisions.

Maybe you decided that a 70% profit margin looks pretty good compared to the 15% margin you would get from the Big 5 Publishers and decided to indie publish your book.

Either way you have a book to write, and writing a book is a project. Publishing a book requires you to perform a variety of tasks with distinct start and end dates in order to produce something unique. This is the very definition of a project as defined by the Project Management Institute, which says a project is a temporary endeavor with distinct start and end dates, undertaken to create a unique product, service or result.[3]

If you sold your manuscript to a traditional publisher, you must write the book by the imposed deadline of the publisher. If you sold a completed manuscript, you must meet revision deadlines, copy edit approval deadlines, etc.

The indie publisher must perform all the tasks previously handled by the traditional publisher in their book project. This includes production tasks such as cover design, copyediting, etc., marketing tasks such as distributing the book to online retailers, bookstores, and libraries; and communication tasks such as launch announcements, book tours, etc.

You might think that if you handle all aspects of writing, publishing, distributing and marketing the book yourself you can avoid having to worry about deadlines. That is true. While no one may impose a deadline on any one of these activities, it is good to set deadlines for yourself. Why? Because you have the GOAL of publishing, not just writing, and to hit the goal you need a deadline.

Why goals need deadlines

You will never achieve your goal of getting your book published if you do not set deadlines for your goal. Why? Because you have a lot of important things to do other than getting your book published. You know the list: you have a day job to-do list, your family to-do list, and odds are several others to-do lists.

If you don't set a deadline for the different stages of finishing a book project, those other non-book tasks will keep interfering in your work. It is that simple. Life will continue to get in the way as you will always tell yourself, that's okay, I can work on the book tomorrow.

I know this is true because, I, like most new writers, had to go through that stage before I published my first book. Oh, you might write books – I wrote four novels and over eighty short stories, but I only published five short stories. Yes, as you may have guessed, those stories were for contests with deadlines!

If you are publishing without using deadlines, then keep doing what you are doing. You have a successful process that works for you, don't mess with it.

However, if you struggle to meet your publishing deadlines, or suspect you might be more successful if you do set deadlines, then keep reading. There is a good chance you will be more productive and more successful if you set deadlines for yourself – even if no one imposes them on you. This book will give you a number of ideas, techniques and tips for improving your ability to set deadlines, write to deadlines and hit deadlines.

Your book project is a balancing act

`Your ability to finish a book is impacted by the amount of Time you have, the Costs involved, and the number of Tasks required to complete your book project.

If you decrease the time available to write your book, you will need to increase the amount of work required to produce the book if you are to maintain the same quality of the book. One option when you get behind on meeting your writing goals is often to outsource some of the work.

The more work performed by others, the higher your cost to produce the book, but the more time you have to write your next book.

Therefore, managing your book project to meet your deadline is a matter of tracking the time you spend working on the book, the amount of work required to complete the book, and the money spent on producing the book.

This relationship between cost, time and tasks is usually represented as:

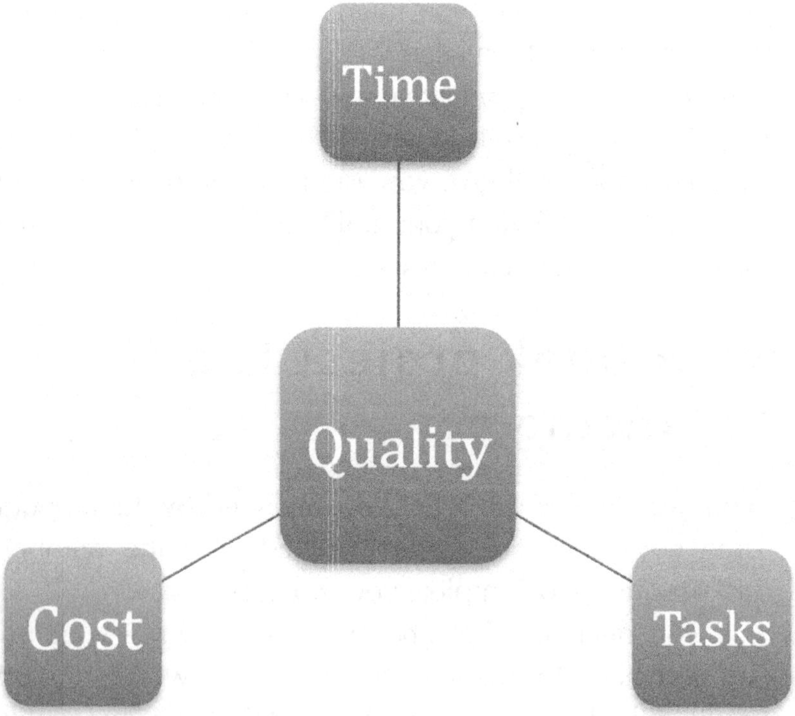

Relationship between Time, Cost and Tasks

Just as you created a business plan to help achieve your business goals, you should also create a plan to make sure you finish your book project on time.

If you are an indie publisher, writing the book represents the first step. You must also create a book cover or hire someone to create one for you. You must either convert the text into the format that is required by your online retailer or hire someone to do the conversion for you.

If you are writing a non-fiction book, you must also make sure your footnotes, indices are correct, and your bibliography is accurate.

A lot goes into writing and publishing a book. These days, even if you are submitting your work to a traditional publisher, much of the editing and marketing falls on the author.

Many writers say that they can't predict how long it will take to write a book before they start writing, but you can come up with a good estimate if you know how fast you write and stick to a schedule.

When you learn know how to track your progress, you can determine whether you are ahead of or behind schedule. You can then work more hours to get caught up if needed in order to meet your deadline.

If you take the time to identify the tasks required to complete your book project and record the time (in days, weeks, or months) needed to complete each task, you will find the accuracy of your time estimates will increase. You can then use your writing history to predict your future writing schedules.

Many writers resist the idea of managing their book projects, thinking that *managing* a creative process will somehow *hurt* the creative process.

If you are worried about the impact of managing your progress against a deadline, think of the two jobs you have: the first is the artist that creates art through writing. The second job you have is the businessperson who must find a buyer for that art, track income and expenses. If you are a self-publisher or indie publisher, you have even more business tasks to accomplish.

The Romantic Suspense novelist, M.L. Buchman and his sister, photographer M.L. Buchman, wrote in their book, *Manage Your Inner Artist/Writer: Strategies For Success,*[4] that you have to get your creative-self and business-self to realize that you will be most successful if both work together.

In this book, I will be talking about the Creative Mind and the Critical Mind. This is the same idea of separating yourself as author and yourself as publisher. Chapter 4 discusses how you can use this concept to prevent the organization and tracking aspects of meeting your deadline from interfering with your creativity.

Tracking the number of words you write, and the money you spend on creating the book might sound boring or scary or both! If you are to succeed as a writing entrepreneur, you need to accept that a certain amount of organization will benefit you. In addition, your business success will allow you to keep doing what you love – writing and creating books.

The five stages of a book project

When you start a book project, you typically go through five stages before your book is complete. These include:

As an indie publisher, I include the production of the book as part of the "writing" or "creating" stage. I break this stage into:

- Writing
- Cover design
- Copy Editing
- Beta Reader Feedback
- Revision
- Interior Book Design
- Publishing
- Distribution

I do not include marketing and communication into this stage since these tasks are ongoing and do not have a distinct end date, but I would include launch tasks and dates.

For now, let's keep the stages simple and just concentrate on the writing of the book. Once you are comfortable meeting your writing deadline, you can add production tasks into these stages or you can set up your production as its own project.

Here is a brief overview of the stages. Later chapters examine each of these stages in more detail:

Stage 1: Starting your book project – This is the idea stage. You may have a number of ideas. You may get multiple book ideas at the same time during this stage! Write them all down and use this stage to determine which project you will start next. Finally, prioritize your book project ideas so that you know which book you will write when this one is completed! You will also be able to research the next book during times when the book maybe in beta reader review, being copy edited, etc.

Stage 2: Planning your book – The planning stage includes research required, trips, the development of your outline, planning how you will use your time, and setting up a schedule for your writing to meet your deadline.

Stage 3: Writing your book – The writing stage includes the hardest part of the project, the most exciting part, and the scariest part. This is the stage that is most affected by procrastination and where most writers make mistakes that force them to miss their deadline.

Stage 4: Managing your book progress – The key to meeting your deadline is the managing stage. If you monitor your progress on a regular basis, you will be able to determine whether you are behind, or ahead of your schedule. Remember, it is possible to adjust your schedule to accommodate unforeseen circumstances and still meet your deadline.

Stage 5: Finishing your book on time and on budget – Finishing your book project includes not just the completion of your writing, but also noting what you learned during the project, to improve your ability to meet book deadlines in the future.

Okay, now that we understand the basic structure of the five stages, we can get into the fun stuff!

NOTE: Writing and Monitoring Stages

During the monitoring stage, you will be going back and forth to the writing stage. That is fine. However, make sure you are not stuck at this stage. Rewriting your book repeatedly often does not improve the quality, especially for beginners who have not learned how to edit their work. Revising can become an excuse for not finishing your book.

CAUTION: Many writers get to the middle of the story or book and begin to think the writing is terrible. They go back and try to fix their work. This is your Critical Mind trying to tell your Creative Mind what to do.

KEEP WRITING! I can't stress enough that this is a common feeling. If you FINISH the book, and go back and read the entire book, you will be amazed at how good your writing was and wonder why you thought it was bad.

If you find yourself in this "fix-it" loop try finishing the first draft of your entire manuscript, then go back and reread your book before allowing yourself to "fix" or "rewrite" the middle of your book.

Top three chapter points to remember

- Publishing a book is a goal and research has shown the best way to achieve a goal is to write it down and monitor progress toward the deadline.
- There are five stages in writing a book:
    1. Idea Generation
    2. Planning
    3. Writing
    4. Monitoring your progress
    5. Finishing
- Expect to cycle between the Planning, Writing and Monitoring stages while working on your book.

Chapter 2: Stage 1 – Developing Your Idea

Getting started on your book

The moment you get an idea for a book and make the decision to write that book, you have started your next book project! This is an exciting time. You have a wonderful idea. The book is forming in your mind and you are anxious to get going.

Characters start appearing in your thoughts at odd moments. Your creative mind can't shut up. You run to your writing space and start jotting down ideas. Enjoy the moment. Protect this creative period from the mundane task of spreadsheets and tracking that can shut down your creativity. Milk that inspiration for as much as you can.

Glory in this **initial stage** of your book project. Many authors dive into planning their book, unable to think of anything besides the tsunami of ideas flooding their brain. They begin their research. They draft character profiles. They start thinking in terms of story arcs. You might worry – and with good reason – that if you start thinking about how to manage your book project at this stage, your Critical Mind might take over and put a stop to your creative momentum.

You don't need to worry – you have *already* started your book project. So let your Creative Mind rush forward at a hundred miles an hour. For once, your Critical Mind can sit back and relax, smug in the knowledge, that even though your Creative Mind doesn't have a clue, all the ideas, all the frantic research, plotting, and character profiles compose the first stage of your book project. So go with the flow and enjoy the moment.

Understanding the first stage of your fiction book project

This first stage of a book project prepares you for the actual writing of the book. As the book becomes clearer to you, you begin to document your thoughts. You form a basic plan for the book.

Those authors who get excited by crafting specific outlines of their upcoming writing projects, love this stage and enjoy setting up spreadsheets with their forecast writing goals, anticipated deadlines, projected costs, and potential revenue as much as the actual writing. If you fall into this category, rejoice. You are going to love managing your book project; but don't rush into your spreadsheets just yet. You need to milk the creative period for all you can.

If you hate spreadsheets, take heart – you do not need them to manage your book project.

TIP: The Value of Spreadsheets

I often read blog posts that criticize books or articles that talk about authors using spreadsheets and I feel bad for writers who have a fear of this essential tool. There are hundreds of spreadsheets that have been created by writers for writers. Even though you can manage a business without spreadsheets, it is easier if you do use them.

Learning how to put together a simple spreadsheet is one of the best skills you can develop for your writing career. Contrary to what many people are saying online, you do not need an MBA to learn how to use a simple spreadsheet and you don't need to be a math whiz.

I get along with spreadsheets just fine, and all I know how to do is basic math with columns and rows.

I have posted an Excel mini-lesson posted on the Business Books For Writers website:

www.businessbooksforwriters.com/Excel_lesson

But I'm warning you: EXCEL is so easy you will wonder why you didn't use it before!

Working with co-authors

If you are working with a co-author, at some point you'll quit kicking ideas around and decide that you are going to do a book together. A lot of decisions led to this point:

- What type of book are you going to write?
- How are you going to work together?
- What is your role vs. co-author's role?
- How often will you communicate?
- How will you communicate (once a week on Google Hangouts; daily with Twitter direct message; a status report on Google docs, https://docs.google.com, or using a project management system for books like Book Planner, www.bookplanner.com, where everything is set up for you or Nozbe, https://nozbe.com, where writers are creating and sharing plans all the time.
- What milestone dates and deadlines will you have for the book?

Both you and your co-author(s) should put the answers to these questions in writing. Then sit down together – in person, if possible; if not, through an online chat or video conference – and talk through these decisions to make sure you share the same expectations regarding the purpose of the book, the way you will work together, what you will deliver to each other, and when you will complete the work. After you have discussed how you will work with your co-author, call a lawyer to write up a contract containing your agreements.

NOTE: You and your co-author need a contract!

If you are working with a co-author, you need to contact an IP lawyer who is experienced drawing up contracts for authors. You can find IP lawyers for writers through professional writing organizations such as Sisters in Crime, www.sistersincrime.org, The Romance Writers of America, www.rwa.org, etc.

Having a contract drawn up will ensure that you and your co-author stay business associates for a long time. A contract is even more important if you and your co-author are related or friends!

Here are just some of the benefits of having a contract:

- Identifies how things will be handled if one of you decides they do not have the time or interest in the project
- States what will happen if either of you dies during the project
- Specifies how the money will be handled
- Clarifies how rights will be handled
- Describes responsibilities if there is a suit brought against the book

A case study – why co-authors and/or partners need a contract

Three friends started a web-based company together. The three were good friends and no one wanted to spend precious investment money on a contract. One of the partners read, you always need a contract when you have partners and pushed for a contract. One of the partners felt that by having a contract, they were saying they didn't trust each other but went along and they had a contract drawn up for the company.

The contract stated what would happen if someone left the company, how revenues would be split, how decisions would be made, etc.

Within three months, the first partner unexpectedly got divorced and moved out of state. According to the company rules, her third of the investment money had to be returned and the two remaining partners had joint ownership of the company.

Two months later the second partner decided to retire and wanted his third of the investment money returned. That meant the remaining partner had sole ownership of the company. Of course, a good bit of the investment money had been spent so that person also had the company debt.

The lone partner worked long hours and the company took off, the profits soared and four months later, a large firm with over 300 employees bought the last partner out.

The second partner now wanted a piece of the profits from the sale of the company, but the contract was very clear that once the original investment had been paid back, the remaining owner(s) kept all future profits and/or revenue from the sale of the company.

My advice: If you are working with another writer, have a contract. It is less expensive than paying for a lawsuit if your book goes viral; Hollywood comes knocking and a dispute erupts about profit sharing and rights.

Working with a traditional publisher

When you work with a traditional publisher, first time authors are typically asked to submit a book proposal. Even previously published authors might be asked to submit a proposal. For those writers who prefer to write without an outline, having to sit down and describe the plot of their book feels like punishment. Many can't wait to reach the level where the publishing house trusts their talent enough that the publisher no longer requires a proposal.

You might consider writing a proposal anyway. The proposal serves the same purpose as documenting the understanding between the co-authors in terms of setting expectations.

I write a book proposal for myself, even when I do not intend to send my books to a traditional publisher. This approach allows me to make sure my author side and my publisher side both understand and agree on what work is required during the book project.

I find my final books have never followed the proposal, but, if I get stuck during the writing stage, having the proposal is a great resource for reminding me what I intended to do with the book. This helps me get through any roadblocks and resume the writing.

Starting your non-fiction book project

Non-fiction writers also get excited about an idea for their new book. Consultants often use book projects to establish their expertise in their consulting or to be required reading for a workshop they conduct.

As with fiction writers, you want to capture all those great ideas that strike during those creative mind tsunamis.

When you reach the point where you have nailed down your idea, it is helpful (after your writing side has had its fun developing the idea) for your publishing side to review these questions before starting to write the book to verify the book can sell:

1) Does your book project fit your short and long-term business strategies?
2) Do you have the budget to complete your project? (Can you afford travel expenses, outsourcing expenses for the cover, copyeditor, proofreader, research, any additional production expenses, marketing expenses, etc.)?
3) Will your existing readers be attracted to this book idea? (i.e., will you be building an audience for your current or planned portfolio of books?

4) Will the book attract a new audience? Why will they be attracted to the book?
5) Why write this book as opposed to other books you might write?
6) Who is involved in the creation of the book? (Research contacts, cover designer, co-author, etc.)
7) What is your backup plan if something prevents you from finishing the book by the deadline?
8) What is the deadline for the book to be finished? (More on this in the next chapter.)

Top three chapter points to remember

- You will have a business advantage if you can do basic math within a simple spreadsheet. You can learn this at the Business Books For Writers website.
- Always hire a lawyer to draw up a contract for you and your co-author.
- Consider writing a book proposal even if you are indie publishing. It will help you in planning your book project.

Chapter 3: Stage 2 - Planning Your Book Schedule

If you are going to set goals for your writing, you are more likely to meet those goals if you write them down according to a research study by Gail Matthews of Dominican University.[5]

Professor Matthews divided 256 study participants into five groups:

- Group 1 – Thought about their goals but did not write them down
- Group 2 – Wrote down their goals
- Group 3 – Wrote down their goals and the actions they would take to achieve their goals
- Group 4 – Wrote down their goals and the actions they would take to achieve their goals and committed to a friend they would achieve their goal
- Group 5 – Wrote down their goals and the actions they would take to achieve their goals, committed to a friend they would achieve their goal and sent progress reports to their friend.

Four weeks later Professor Matthews analyzed the student's performance and concluded in her research summary:

- Those in Group 5 who sent weekly progress reports to their friend accomplished significantly more than those who had not written down their goals.
- Those in Group 1 who did not write down their goals had the lowest success rate of reaching their goal.

Writing down your goals greatly increases your chances of achieving your goals. If you want to complete your book project by a deadline you need to write down the deadline, commit to making the deadline and be willing to hold yourself accountable to making the deadline and tracking your progress toward reaching your goal.

Setting up a schedule for your book project

During the first stage of working on your book project, you decided what you wanted to write, or at least developed a basic idea. During the project, you need to know how you are doing in meeting your deadline.

TIP: You Don't Need To Know What You Will Write

Managing the process of meeting your deadline does not mean you need to know everything you will write before you start. You can write without an outline as many writers do, but still monitor your progress and learn what to do when you are either behind or ahead of your schedule.

One method of determining whether you are ahead or behind your deadline is tracking the words you have written. You can then set dates by which you plan to have a chapter written or a specific number of words written. These dates are called Milestone dates. If you have not reached your goal by the milestone date, you know you need to work harder on subsequent days to meet your deadline. This gives you the confidence to know you can catch up and still make your deadline and eliminates the stress of realizing you only have a week before your project is due and there is no way you can finish.

When your main character's best buddy shows up unexpectedly in your book and takes over the plot, you can adjust your writing goals if you have a tracking plan. If you don't have a plan, you only know your 80,000 word book just added 20,000 words you never intended to write. Often, this is when you look at the calendar and begin panicking and wondering how in the world you will finish by your deadline.

Understanding your task list

Chapter 1 described how a project must balance time, number of tasks (called scope) and cost. In order to meet your deadline, you need to know what tasks you need to complete by your deadline and how long it will take to complete those tasks, even if you are just guessing.

You can set up your task plan by creating a picture of the different tasks you need to complete to write, produce, and publish your book or by making a simple list of the tasks required. Two approaches are presented, but writers typically develop their own approach. If you start writing projects without documenting the steps, and you need to complete your writing project, try one or both of these approaches.

NOTE: Only use the ideas that work for you

If you try an idea and it doesn't work for you, try something else. Don't quit trying to learn how you can best manage your book projects, because one idea didn't work.

Create a spreadsheet listing the tasks involved in writing your book

You can also list your tasks on paper in the order you would do them. Most people will find it easier to put this task list into a spreadsheet like Excel or Google Sheets. Using a spreadsheet has the advantage of allowing you to record when you start the task and when you complete the task in columns associated with the task. You can easily reorder tasks or create calculations such as total time remaining until your deadline.

Step 1: Open the spreadsheet where you listed the tasks you need to complete for your book project. Enter your estimates for time to complete the tasks in the spreadsheet with the tasks listed on the left (rows) and either days or weeks listed horizontally (columns).

Step 2: Identify which tasks require other tasks to be completed before they can start. For example, you need to finish writing your book before you can send the manuscript to your copyeditor. Identifying which tasks are dependent on other tasks, and which tasks can be done simultaneously, helps you coordinate your work so that no task is ignored. Examples of simultaneous tasks would be "write Chapter 3" and "request cover design." Both tasks can be done during the same week. This allows you to have the book completed at the same time the cover design is finalized, eliminating any delays in the launch of the book.

Step 3: After you list your tasks and identify which are dependent on each other and which can be done simultaneously, assign an estimate of how long it will take you to complete each task. (If you are new to estimating times for writing a book, use your best guess.) Add additional days to any tasks that you have never done before or that carry a greater risk of not being completed within your estimated amount of time. This will cover any "contingencies" or unanticipated delays that might arise.

Step 4: Add up the number of days it will take you to complete all the tasks.

Step 5: Once you total the amount of time required to complete your project, see if the number of days to complete the tasks you listed are less than the total time you have to complete the project. This is the amount of time that your project can be delayed and still make its deadline.

If a chapter takes longer to write than you anticipated, or it takes longer to finish a task than you originally guessed, you can use some of this extra time to finish that chapter or do the time-consuming tasks, and still stay on schedule.

If you finish a task sooner than you thought, you can add the time you didn't need into your available time to use if a future task takes longer than expected.

Book project flow charts – a visual aid

You can also create a visual diagram of each task, ordering the tasks as they flow from one to another in a flow chart diagram. Some people hate flow chart diagrams. Some people love them. You don't have to use them but they can be useful in identifying duplicate or forgotten steps in your process.

Once you develop a flow chart that represents the tasks you typically do when you write a book, you will not need to develop a flow chart for every subsequent book. However, you might decide to develop a diagram for each *type* of book you write, if your writing process differs between genres or if you write fiction and non-fiction.

Flow chart examples

I like flowcharts because I can see the steps I need to take to complete my book project. There are other ways to list the time you allot to required tasks, but the key to hitting your deadline is to know the steps or tasks you plan to follow and write them down. I say 'plan to follow,' because the final book rarely matches the plan the author originally designed. That is why you adjust your plan during the project. Don't be afraid of making changes to your plan and don't forget to document the changes you made so you remember them when you work on your next book project.

Examples of two flow charts

The first example is the flow chart I use when writing a book. The second example is of an indie publishing flow chart I created for writing and producing a non-fiction book.

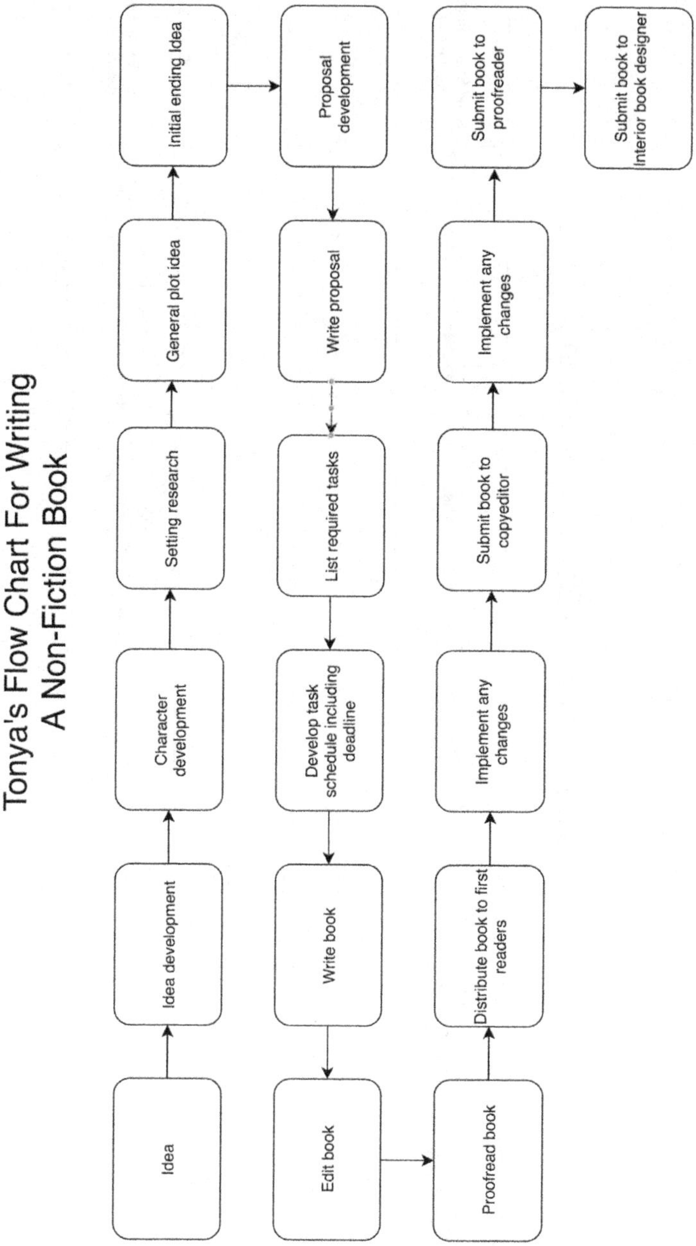
Tonya's Flow Chart For Writing
A Non-Fiction Book
Idea
Idea development
Character development
Setting research
General plot idea
Initial ending idea
Proposal development
Write proposal
List required tasks
Develop task schedule including deadline
Write book
Edit book
Proofread book
Distribute book to first readers
Implement any changes
Submit book to copyeditor
Implement any changes
Submit book to proofreader
Submit book to Interior book designer

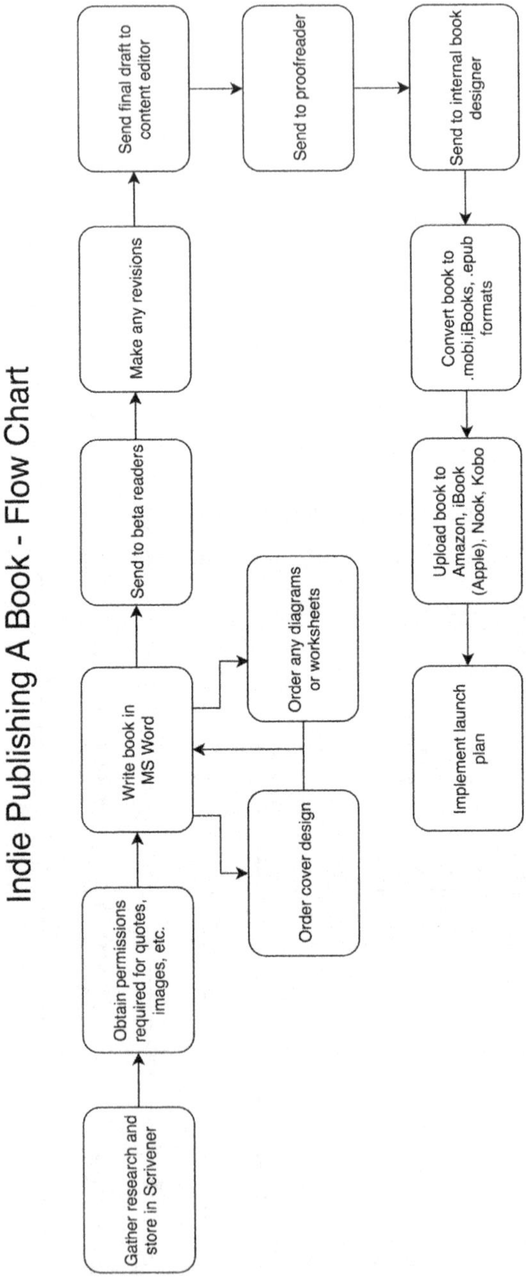
Indie Publishing A Book - Flow Chart
Gather research and store in Scrivener
Obtain permissions required for quotes, images, etc.
Write book in MS Word
Order cover design
Order any diagrams or worksheets
Send to beta readers
Make any revisions
Send final draft to content editor
Send to proofreader
Send to internal book designer
Convert book to .mobi,iBooks, .epub formats
Upload book to Amazon, iBook (Apple), Nook, Kobo
Implement launch plan

If you look at this and think that this would add nothing for your writing process, then don't create a flow chart. It is presented as something that might be useful. If it isn't, don't bother with it.

If you do like this approach, you can experiment with creating your own flowcharts. I use Draw.IO's online Flowchart Maker, www.draw.io. It is free and easy to use.

The Business Books For Writers website has examples of several flow charts writers might use. Do you have a flowchart you want to share with this book's readers? Just email TPrice@TonyaPrice.com and she'll add your example to the web page.

Over time you may change your process, either because you find better ways to write your books or because the industry changes. That's not a problem. Just update your flowchart. You can use your flowchart to help you remember each step in creating your book. Following the flowchart guarantees you won't skip a step in your process.

You don't need to use flowcharts, but you do need to write down your task list and assign approximate times to complete each task if you want to track your progress as you write.

As you complete each task, record the amount of time you actually spent. Then, use those actuals as your estimates for your next book. Over time, the accuracy of your estimates will improve.

Will some of your estimates fall short of the actual time needed? Absolutely.

However, you will also find you will overestimate other tasks. In fact, in the next chapter you will learn a trick for adding time to your estimate in order to make sure you hit your deadline.

In the end, you want to develop the ability to get better at predicting the total time you need to write (and for indie publishers, publish) your book. But it all starts with creating your book project schedule.

TIP: Improving your task estimates over time

You will probably not be very accurate the first time you try to estimate how long it will take you to accomplish your tasks, but by documenting the time you take you will improve over time.

If you fear that estimating tasks times will make it impossible to write, then list start and end dates each day. When the book is done, and there is no more pressure to finish writing, then go back and write down how long each task took to complete.

Top three chapter points to remember

- When you assign yourself a writing deadline, make a commitment to hitting that deadline, share your deadline with others and track your progress, you are more likely to complete your book before your deadline.

- Identify the tasks required to completing your book. You can write your task list in MS Word, on paper, in a spreadsheet or using a flow chart. There are other ways to identify and track your tasks. Find the way that works best for you.
- Once you have identified the tasks you need to complete to finish your book project, estimate how long it will take you to complete your task. Don't worry if your estimates are wrong, you are learning to get better at predicting your estimates for the future.

Chapter 4: Stage 3 – Writing Your Book

In the Introduction, we discussed the idea that writers have a *Creative Mind* and a *Critical Mind*. Your Creative Mind likes to invent things like interesting characters, unusual settings, and unusual conflicts, and play with what happens. Your Creative Mind asks "what if" continuously. Your Creative Mind represents your imagination and your ideas. Your Creative Mind must be nurtured and protected.

Your Critical Mind keeps you organized. Your Critical Mind loves grammar and rules. Your Critical Mind understands goal setting, strategies, and the need to hit financial goals. Your Critical Mind can shut down your Creative Mind by its propensity to criticize all the fun stuff your Creative Mind invents.

You can't let this happen. You need to set up rules for your Critical Mind. Yes, you will need to unleash your critical thinking skills, but only after the Creative Mind has told wonderful tales with fascinating characters set in imaginary worlds.

The Critical Mind will rarely approve of the Creative Mind's work. Don't pay attention to the Critical Mind's opinion of the quality of the story you tell. Set up boundaries, and force the two sides of your mind to stay on their own sides. The Critical Mind should only be allowed to focus on the business side of your work, and must stay out of the creative process. Some authors go so far as to do their creative writing in one room on one computer, and keep their business work confined to another room on a separate computer.

Recognize that to be an indie publisher you need to cultivate and value both the Creative Mind and the Critical Mind. The writer and the businessperson. Both are valuable. Both are required for your business success.

The author that indulges the Creative Mind and disparages the Critical Mind will fail just as quickly as the author that lets the Critical Mind dominate over the Creative Mind.

Authors are not alone in this, by the way. Almost every entrepreneur has to wrangle with the boundaries between creativity and critical thinking. Your skill at balancing creativity and critical thinking will determine your success as a writing entrepreneur.

This balance between the Creative Mind and the Critical Mind scares many writers. They worry that if they start tracking words written and time spent writing, they will no longer be able to write and that could lead to the dreaded writer's block.

Everyone has to determine for themselves how best to control these two opposite, but invaluable aspects of the writing process.

I deal with the fear that my Critical Mind will shut down my Creative Mind by always putting my writing first. Only after I have written for the day, do I document and evaluate my progress toward meeting my deadline.

At the end of my writing time, I let my Creative Mind to rest and I unleash my Critical Mind. I don't review the book in progress. Instead, I limit my Critical Mind to such mundane tasks as noting how many words I wrote. How many hours did I write? Did I incur any unexpected costs? What new emails have arrived?

You might have a different approach. Some writers follow a strict outline. These can get very detailed. I've talked to authors who break the outline into how many words each chapter should contain.

This book deals with Critical Mind thinking. I don't pretend to tell you how to write better stories. You are busy and have a lot of information to deal with and things to do, so this book focuses on how to meet your book's deadline. Nothing else.

So, let's look at some methods of determining your progress against your deadline, and how to deal with various issues that might impact your ability to finish your book on time.

You can't hit your goal if you don't know where you are

In order to know how you are doing in meeting your deadline, you have to know how many words you have written. Luckily, you can track your word count with little effort. If you write in Microsoft Word, you get a count of words by going to the Tools tab and selecting "Word Count." You can also see the word count at the bottom of the Word file window. Other writing programs, such as Scrivener, have similar word count features.

Fancy programs exist for tracking your daily word count, but you don't need them. A simple spreadsheet works as well.

Keep your writing record as simple or as complicated as you wish. Log the number of words you have written at the start of your writing time and the number you completed at the end of the day. Chapter 5 – Monitoring your book project talks about this in greater detail.

TIP: Developing a habit

If you have never tracked your word count, you might find it hard to start. It is easiest to get started if you use a template. You can find one at the Business Books For Writers Examples

www.businessbooksforwriters.com/examples

I update my sheet at the start and end of my business day. When I started I often forgot, but remember: if you do something every day for three weeks, you form a habit. Once you develop the habit of starting and ending your day with your word count, (I include hours too) then you get a real sense of accomplishment!

At the end of the year, you will be astounded by how much you have accomplished even if you only write 250 words a day, in 365 days you will have written 91,250 words! That is an 80,000-word novel plus revisions. If you write 1000 words a day, in 365 days you will have written 4.5 novels!

Track your word count and prove to yourself you are getting things done!

Accept that there will be times when you will not write as fast as at other times. For me this typically happens at the middle of a novel or a short story. This great idea I had, that I knew would win awards, suddenly seems the most commonplace plot in the world and the characters the stupidest idiots to ever inhabit a page.

If that happens to you, just keep writing. When the book is done, the writing in the middle of the book will amaze you.

Don't get depressed by your speed. Typically, when you hit the last fourth of the book, your speed will crank up. Rather than get hung up on your words per day or even words per week track your general progress.

Science Fiction author Ron Collins http://typosphere.com, no longer tracks his word count, but tracks the hours in his chair writing instead. Use whatever metric you are most comfortable with, but use some measure to allow you to determine how you are progressing toward your project's deadline.

How to know if you are behind schedule

New authors often don't realize they are behind schedule until they are just a couple of weeks from their deadline.

This inability to recognize that the project cannot be completed in time comes from inexperience in tracking your writing pace. If you are working on your first novel, you have no way of knowing how long you normally take to complete a chapter, or even how fast you write.

Traditional publishers often only accept completed novels from new authors, because they know the authors have not developed the ability to predict the time they require to complete a chapter, let alone an entire book.

If you are a first-time author planning to self-publish your book consider completing your book before you schedule your book's copy editor, cover designer, and proofreader. This takes the pressure off you to meet a string of committed deadlines.

Don't waste this opportunity, learn to estimate your productivity! Go ahead and track the amount of words you write each day, and create a deadline for yourself. When you finish your book, your word count per day will help you create a more realistic deadline for your next book.

Continue this habit with every book and you will get very good at predicting your writing speed.

Monitoring your word count will alert you early that you are falling behind in your schedule. But how do you catch up? There are a number of options available. Review each one, and then determine which will work best for the type of book you're writing and the circumstances you face. And don't be afraid to invent new options based on the way you write.

More strategies for meeting your deadlines

The Writer's Business Plan stated the key to success in indie publishing is your *inventory* – the number of books you have for sale. Let's say that you set as a business goal to write four novels a year, each approximately 60,000 words long. That is 240,000 words a year. You would have three months, or sixty workdays to write each book. That works out to 1000 finished words a day.

If you write 2000 words a day, you will complete the book in 30 workdays, and will have an additional 30 days for tasks such as sending the book to your first readers, making edits, having the book proof read, the interior layout done, etc. Chances are, you will write 3000 words some days and 500 words other days. Tracking the number of words you complete each day will signal if you are behind or ahead in your word count.

If you are delayed, and one of your tasks takes two extra days, you will still finish on time with eight days to spare if you put extra time for contingencies into your original estimate of time required to complete that task.

Likewise, if you estimate it will take ten days to complete your edits, and you finish them in five days, then you have fifteen extra days that can be used on tasks that take longer than you expected. There are many ways you can meet your deadlines, even if you experience delays that are beyond your control. Let's look at some of these strategies.

Write out of order

Roger Parker, in an article for Activegarage.com published January 23, 2013 titled, "Finishing your book on time and avoiding writers block,"[6] recommended keeping your writing on schedule by writing out of order. Rather than write the story from beginning to end, he talks about writing the "easy" parts first. He goes on to say that you don't even have to finish a chapter, just write those parts that come naturally. He adds two caveats: Finish your first draft, then edit. He also notes that once you start writing, you will pick up speed as you go along.

I use to find this approach difficult to implement, but I know a number of authors who write out of order with great success. Recently, I have found that if I get stuck in the plot, writing the ending helps me figure out what to do with the middle of the novel. Consider trying this if your writing bogs down or if the ending suddenly comes to you while you are writing.

If you find yourself stuck in a novel, don't quit. Don't even walk away for a few days. Keep writing. Experiment with writing out of order. If you experience difficulties writing out of order, then try writing something else, but *don't quit writing*. Any forward progress will help get you back on track.

Cut out a subplot

Stephen King in his book, "On Writing"[7] talks about the advantage of cutting out 10% of your first draft to improve your book. If you find yourself up against a deadline, examine your book to see if there is a subplot, you might eliminate in order to complete the book on time. Is there a minor character who has started to take over the plot? Maybe you can save them for a sequel.

You don't want to edit to reduce your word count just to meet a deadline, but consider sitting back and analyzing the book-to-date to see if eliminating a minor subplot that does little for the story can reduce your writing time.

Analyze what might be interfering with your writing time

Distractions suck up writing hours. If you find yourself behind on your writing schedule, look for any time sinks that are diverting you from making your word count. If you do not already have a set writing time, try establishing one. I write full time, so I am at my desk at 8:00 a.m. every day. I write in the morning. During this time, I usually get in about 3000 words and a couple of breaks. At noon, I eat lunch, and at 12:30, I do business tasks and work another four hours.

I don't worry if I don't make my word count goal every day; but if I find myself behind by several days or a week, I eliminate the afternoon routine and get in four hours of extra writing. On those days, I write from 8:00 a.m. until noon, and again from 1:00 p.m. until 4:00, for a total of seven hours writing time. Those extra three hours help me catch up.

In a pinch, I can push myself and write for ten to twelve hours at a stretch, but that pace can exhaust you and lead to burnout, so you don't want to make that your routine.

Everyone needs a backup plan for those situations when you are behind, and time sinks such as TV time, reading time, and Internet surfing time are distractions you can eliminate from your daily routine when you see yourself getting behind.

Have your writing buddy keeps you accountable

In *The Writer's Business Plan,* we mentioned if you don't have a writing buddy, find one. A spouse, a reader, or a fellow writer can serve as a writing buddy. Writing buddies do not have to live near you. Many people connect online. You can meet them in writing workshops, in online groups or through networking.

When you find yourself lagging behind, let your writing buddy know. They will offer encouragement. They probably know your writing habits better than you do, and can offer suggestions on how to catch up to your writing goal.

Writing buddies often just lend support, but they can also spot ways you may be sabotaging your own productivity. Listen to them. Don't get angry at them, even when you don't want to hear what they have to say. Think about their advice. You can always ignore them. But you should respect them for having the courage to say what you may not want to hear!

When it comes to procrastination and distractions, we usually know our guilty pleasures. Sometimes, we really need that true writing friend who will tell us what we know deep inside, but haven't been able to admit to ourselves, to help get us back on track.

Write faster

Writing faster requires extra effort. The easiest way to write faster is to eliminate those things that stop you from writing or slow you down.

Do you stop to check email? Limit your email reading to your lunch break, and then you have hit your daily writing goal.

Are you interrupted by telephone calls? Turn off the ringer during your writing hours.

Do you work at home? Let your friends know that you don't answer calls or the door during your writing hours and then don't answer the phone! If you work with family members at home, then talk to them about coming up with a plan that will give you uninterrupted writing time.

Another way to write faster is to use an outline. You don't need to strictly follow the outline, but you can use an outline to get you started, and when you find yourself stuck, your outline can remind you of your overall goal or theme. Often, just reviewing an outline can give you an idea you didn't consider before.

Many authors prefer to write without an outline. If you write without an outline and get stuck, write a short, quick outline that just covers the next chapter or even next scene. You may be surprised at how this helps you get going on those days when you sit down and struggle to get words down.

Family commitments can throw off a writing schedule more than anything else. Don't underestimate the difficulty of writing at home with small children. Do remember, though, children grow up quickly and change constantly.

You, your kids and your writing will be better if you spend time with your kids. You will have plenty of time by yourself soon enough so work around their schedule. Write when they are in bed, and if they get up, adjust.

Authors who write at home need to learn to write fast. If you can learn to do this while you have young children at home, you gain the benefits even more when you are an empty nester with an entire day to yourself to write!

There are classes you can take to learn to write faster. WMG Publishing offers a good one, called "Speed," taught online by Dean Wesley Smith, www.wmgpublishing workshops.com/how-to-sign-up.

Michael Pollack's blog post, "12 Tips on How to Become a Faster Writer,"[8] offers several good ideas on how to increase your writing speed. Pollack recommends knowing what you are going to write before you start. When you find yourself behind on your book project, experiment with being more purposeful in your daily writing. Determine what you want to accomplish for that day, and don't stop for the day until you reach your writing goal.

You won't increase your speed overnight, so concentrate on developing this skill over time. Have a target writing speed in mind. Then investigate various ways to increase your speed, and practice to reach this goal.

Want more ideas on how to increase your writing speed? Here are several books that will help you:

5,000 Words Per Hour: Write Faster, Write Smarter: Write Faster, Write Smarter by Chris Fox[9]

Write Better, Faster: How To Triple Your Writing Speed and Write More Every Day (Growth Hacking For Storytellers #1) by Monica Leonelle[10]

2k to 10k: Writing Faster, Writing Better, and Writing More of What You Love by Rachel Aaron[11]

Dictation

Many writers use dictation to increase their speed. While you won't be able to turn to dictation the first time you find your book project behind schedule, if you take the time to learn to write using dictation now, you will increase your writing speed for the future.

I have not developed this skill, but if you want to learn more about this new trend, there are couples of books that can guide you on how to proceed.

Dictate Your Book: How To Write Your Book Faster, Better, and Smarter (Growth Hacking For Storytellers #4) by Michelle Leonelle[12] (Listen to Joanna Penn's podcast with Michelle Leonelle, or read the transcript to hear how to write faster using dictation.)

Dictation: Dictate Your Writing – Write Over A Million Words A Year Without Breaking A Sweat by Kevin Gise[13]

Develop self-discipline

Writing takes self-discipline. Your ability to meet your deadline and achieve success depends on your ability to develop a routine of writing, ignoring distractions, and producing new words on a consistent basis.

Inevitably, you will encounter delays. Your 60,000 – 80,000-word book can handle a few setbacks. Armed with the habit of writing every day, no matter your writing style, you can meet your deadlines.

Have a backup plan for when you get behind. If you struggle to stay on track, don't give up. Keep writing. Put in the time, and you will find yourself increasing your writing consistency.

Dealing with procrastination

I know writers can overcome procrastination, because I used to be so good at putting everything off – and now it is not a problem for me.

If you struggle with procrastination, first make sure that your issue is not committing to so many projects and tasks in your business, family, and social life that you struggle to get everything done. The solution to handling a to-do list is the subject of the third book in the *Business Books For Writers* series: *Completing the Writer's To-do list,* and I mention it here because overbooking yourself with projects is not the same as putting off starting a project.

If however, you are not over-committed and you simply keep finding excuses not to write, or if you get sidetracked by other unimportant, but interesting activities such as television, computer games, etc., then you need to learn to develop strategies for keeping yourself on track.

Here are some tips to help you:

1) Ask yourself why you are having trouble starting your book project and compile the reasons into a list. Taking the time to understand what might be behind your inability to sit at your desk and start writing will help you get over the fear that you cannot overcome your procrastination. Gaining insight into why you procrastinate will help you come up with your own strategies for avoiding work.
2) Set up a writing schedule, and follow it. Experts say that it takes three weeks to develop a habit. If you want to beat your procrastination, give yourself three weeks of following your desired schedule every workday. Just getting in the habit of going to your work desk and writing will help you overcome procrastination. Sure you may have to pitch what you have written, (although it may turn out to be great), but once you develop the habit of sitting at your desk and writing, the procrastination will become less of an issue.
3) List the tasks you need to accomplish to meet your deadline. Doing so helps you manage your project. Your large book project will seem more manageable and less intimidating. When you simplify tasks into smaller components, you focus on doable objectives for each day. This can help you avoid the fear of failure that every author faces when working on a book project. Fear of failure is a major reason people procrastinate.

4) The great thing about tasks is the sense of accomplishment that comes with being able to mark them as done. Sure, you might miss a writing task deadline as you struggle to get into your story, but once you get going, hitting your deadlines will become easier. Focus on that sense of accomplishment you gain as you check one task after another off your list as a way to fight procrastination.

5) Create a productive writing environment. Analyze what in your writing environment might cause you to get distracted, and prevent you from starting your writing for the day. Make changes to eliminate that distraction. Have kids? Write when they are not in the house. Do you get distracted by computer games? Get a separate computer for your writing, and don't load any games on it. Do you get off track because you're constantly checking your email? Turn off the internet on your computer. For any tempting distraction, there is a way for you to control your environment. You just need to identify what keeps you from writing and come up with a strategy to eliminate that distraction.

6) Don't be intimidated by the desire to write the Great American Novel. You don't need to write the Great American Novel, you just need to write the best novel you can. It may never sell. Orit may sell a lot; but even if it does, chances are someday you will write a novel that doesn't sell. That doesn't mean you are a bad writer. You may not be Shakespeare, but Shakespeare would have a hard time selling in today's market

anyway. If you suffer from the need to write the Great American Novel, give yourself permission to write a small book first. You will find it easier to write, and chances are it will be a better story.

7) Eliminate 'I can't do this' from your vocabulary. You may not have learned to do something, but you can learn to do whatever you want to learn. Unless you refuse to try to learn. No successful person ever uttered the word "Can't." Be on the alert whenever you start thinking that you can't track information in spreadsheets or can't track daily word counts. Instead, create a motivating mantra for yourself, such as, "I said I was going to write 1000 words today. Even if I only write 500, I'm going to at least start on the 1000," Or my favorite. "I'm going to try and if I fail, I'm going to try again until I can do this."

8) When you achieve your goal for the day, stop and reward yourself with something you enjoy doing. Creating balance in your life is an important method of avoiding procrastination. I will warn you though, M. L. Buchman has a great line in his book warning writers not to celebrate with food unless you want to gain a lot of weight![14]

9) If you are finding it hard to start writing, check on whether you made your goals for the day too hard to achieve. You want to set yourself up for success not failure.

10) If you are distracted by emails or social media, incorporate them into your motivational tools. Work

for a set amount of time and then allow yourself to take a break for email or social media. I like to use the Pomodoro method where you work for 20 minutes and then take a 5-minute break. During the break you get a reward for sticking with your writing. Now you can check your email, surf etc., but just for five minutes. When I get behind on my writing, I work for 45 minutes before taking a 10-minute break. There are a number of focused timers that are available for your desktop and mobile device to help you track your time. The Zapier website has a good article on several Pomodoro timer apps, https://zapier.com/blog/best-pomodoro-apps, that let you set your work time and break time. If you struggle with distractions, I highly recommend the Pomodoro method to help you avoid distractions, no matter which app you use. I list some Pomodoro and provide more detail in Chapter 8, "Tools To Help You Meet Your Deadlines."

Strategies for those with a full-time job

Almost all writers worked a day job to pay the rent and grocery bills at some point in their life. If you are working full time, consider writing in "time boxes."

Time boxes are fixed amount of time in which you set out to accomplish a specific task.

For example, at one point in my high tech career, I had an hour commute into Boston each morning and a return trip each night. Because I lived at the end of the commuter line and took the train into the beginning station, I always had a seat on the train.

I set up a one-hour time box to write. This one-hour block of time was not enough time to write a chapter, but it was enough time to write a scene, sometimes two.

When I got home each night, I had dinner and then had another two-hour block of time before I went to bed. My goal was to write a thousand words an hour during this time each day. On Saturday and Sunday, I had a four-hour block of time each day to write. By identifying and using these time boxes, I was able to write a minimum of 10,000 words per week and on good weeks, 15,000. (18 hours x 1000 words/hour.)

Day jobs can really throw off a writing schedule. Here is a tip shared by the full-time writer and Derringer nominee, Ron Collins, (#1 on Amazon's UK Dark Fantasy list, #2 in the US).

To avoid having the day job interfere with Ron's writing schedule when he was working full time at a day job he would get up two hours early to write before going to work. That way, he always got in his writing time.

This is a great strategy if you can do it because it tells your Creative Mind it is important and gets priority and it helps you see yourself as a writer that is working a day job, rather than a Project Manager that writes.

You can quite a lot done in Time Boxes.

If you are going to be writing using time boxes, you might want to check out the app, "Timebox." You log your task, and then set the amount of time you have to do that task. If you don't complete the task in the time box, don't worry, just set a new Timebox. This can be a very effective approach to use in doctor's offices, sitting in the car during the kid's soccer practices, etc.

Top three chapter points to remember

- The writer has to nurture their Creative Mind while writing. The indie publisher has to nurture their Critical Mind when working on the business side of publishing. Successful writers get the two to work together.
- You can't hit a deadline if you don't know where you are in your process. Track how many words you have written, but find a way to do this that fits the way you write.
- There are a number of strategies to help you when you get behind. If you track your progress, then you will have time to catch up and meet your deadline.

Chapter 5: Stage 4 – Managing Your Project

Keeping your book project on track

As stated in the previous chapter, in order to meet your book final project deadline, you have to know which tasks you have accomplished and which tasks remain, and how much time you need to finish these tasks. You also need to know your deadline.

One easy way to track your progress if you are not comfortable using spreadsheets is to use a large whiteboard mounted on your office wall. Enter your tasks on the board, assign target due dates for each task, and record the number of words written each day. This approach has the advantage of being a constant reminder to keep writing and works well if your task is not too long.

You can also keep a list of tasks in a simple spreadsheet with a column for tasks, one for estimated time to complete the task and a column to indicate if the task has been finished.

The Gantt Chart

You can also use an excellent tool for tracking your progress called the Gantt chart. Named for Henry Gantt in the early 1900s[15] a Gantt chart is a nice visual aid that indicates if you need to push harder to finish a book, or if you are ahead of schedule.

Note: You can download this *Gantt chart* template

Download from the *Business Books For Writer's* Resource page under Templates for writers.

www.BusinessBooksForWriters.com/Resources

Explanation of the Gantt chart

A Gantt chart may appear a bit intimidating at first, but they are not that complicated. Note that there are different ways you can show planned and actual days for a task; the format presented here is the method I use.

In the Gantt chart for the *Meeting the Writer's Deadline* book project, each cell represents five working or one work week. If you have a day job, one cell might represent the amount of time you have each day to write.

Chart 1: Gantt chart for *Meeting the Writer's Deadline*

Gantt Chart Example										
Tasks	Days allocated for each task									
	Days 1-5	Days 6-11	Days 12 - 17	Days 18 - 23	Days 24-29	Days 30-35	Days 36-41	Days 42-47	Days 48-53	Continues
Idea dev.	5 days									
Research		5 days								
Writing										
Ch. 1			2 days							
Ch. 2			3 days							
Ch. 3				2 days						
Ch. 4				3 days						
Ch.r 5					2 days					
Ch. 6					2 days					
Ch. 7					1 day	1 day				
Ch. 8						2 days				
Resources						2 days				
Bio, etc.							3 days			
Edits								5 days		
Proofread									5 days	
NOTE: This list continues for the length of the project through production										

The first task listed on the chart is *Idea development*. The cell next to the task title contains the words "5 days". This shows that the estimated idea development section of the book will be completed in 5 workdays.

The number of days allocated to the chapters depends on the task to be accomplished. In this example, some chapters are estimated to be written in two days and others are estimated to be written in three days. When two chapters can be completed in one week, they occupy the same column.

How to estimate the time you will need to write your book

Here are four steps you can use to set a writing task deadline:

1) Estimate approximately, how many words or chapters you plan to write.
2) Identify the number of days required to accomplish your goal.
3) After you have listed all your tasks and assigned the estimated number of days, it will take you to finish each task... Add up the time estimates and you will have an estimate of how long it will take to write the entire book.
4) NOW, take all of your estimates and add more days than you think you will need to complete more complex tasks. This builds extra time into the schedule.

Everyone has a different idea of how much extra time they will need for complex tasks. When I have no idea how long a task will take, I guess and double my estimate if there is time! I write very fast so for me this might mean if I have estimated it will take me one week to write a chapter, I will allocate two weeks. I do adjust this approach. If I estimate a chapter would take a month, I might only add two weeks extra time.

You will get better at estimating the more practice you have. Sometimes you have a tight deadline and can't add extra time, but whenever you can, give yourself more days for each task than you think you will need. If your original estimates were close, you'll finish early. This extra time will come in handy if you get behind and will be the key to meeting your deadline.

An alternative method of determining how to meet your writing task deadline is:

1) Calculate the number of days between when you plan to start writing and your assigned writing deadline.
2) Estimate the total number of words you need to write.
3) Divide the number of words by the number of days to determine how many words per day you must write to complete your writing task on time.
4) If you don't hit your daily word count, then you know you need to write more words – either over the next few sessions, or as a new average going forward – to put you back on schedule.

5) Don't forget you still need to assign time for developing your book idea, editing and revisions, and any time required for your team members tasks. Make sure you account for these tasks. if you are an indie publisher you also need to include tasks such as: cover design, blurbs, editing, administrative chores like preparing your business taxes.

If your publisher tells you on May 20 that the due date for your manuscript is Dec 20, you have 8 months, or approximately 160 workdays, to finish your book. Let's say you need one month (20 work days) to complete your research. This leaves you with 140 workdays to write the book.

If you normally write 1000 words per day, at that rate, you would finish a 60,000-word novel in 60 days. You would then have 80 days for editing, revising, proofreading, sending to beta readers, etc.

WARNING: You Must Write

You must write using a consistent schedule or you won't meet your deadline no matter how many lists, spreadsheets, or flow charts you create. If you're struggling with writing daily, see Chapter 4 on "Dealing with procrastination."

Now the exciting part of adding extra time and Gantt charts comes into play!

Say your schedule shows the next task, editing, is starting a day late. If the remaining tasks require all the time originally estimated, and you have used the extra days you calculated were needed to complete your book project, you will finish a day late. However, if even one task finishes one day early, the book project will be finished on time!

You can "catch up" when a project gets behind. By estimating high on how long you need to finish a task, you build extra time into your project for any unforeseen issues that might come up (new ideas, a sick day, a request for a guest blog article, etc.) You might estimate wrong on one task, but few people guess low on every task. You will usually discover that you can finish some tasks earlier than planned. In the end, you want your estimates to balance out, or even better, find you have extra time you didn't need for your book project. Then you finish early!

TIP: Extra time or contingency time has benefits

Over estimating the time to complete a task builds extra time into your schedule and removes the stress from meeting deadlines, allows you to sleep at night, enjoy your life and establish a reputation as a writer who can be counted on to deliver projects on time.

How to show if a task finished early or late on a Gantt Chart

One of the great things about a Gantt Chart is you can show the status of a project, including if a task is late, or finished early. In the chart below predicted tasks are shown as well as actual times to complete the task. Using color codes, you can represent this on one line, but here we are showing the information in multiple lines to illustrate the information.

You can see that Idea Development only took two days to complete, finishing three days early. This allows Research travel, which was estimated to start on day 6 to start on day 3. Research travel requires six days to complete. By starting three days earlier than projected, Research travel ends on its originally finish day. Research travel was scheduled to end on day 8 and in fact, does end on day 8, putting the book project back on schedule.

GANNT Chart Extra Time Example									
	DAYS								
TASKS	1	2	3	4	5	6	7	8	9
Idea Development - predicted	5 days estimated								
Idea Development - actual	**Takes 2 days**		***Finished 3 days early***						
Research, travel - predicted			5 days estimated				***ORIGINAL END DATE***		
Research, travel - actual			***Takes 6 days - Finishes on time Day 8***						

Keep your Gantt chart up to date

Be sure to update your Gantt chart when you finish a task. I have followed this practice for years.

Updating and referring to your Gantt chart often benefits you in three ways:

1) Reviewing your progress reinforces the importance of working towards your goal. If you get behind, you know you need to work harder while there is time to catch up and make your deadline.
2) When you are ahead of your schedule, you feel a motivating sense of accomplishment.
3) If you are ever audited by the IRS, having these daily records will help support your claim that you are seriously pursuing your writing. Having documentation of your writing times lets you prove you are taking a professional approach to your writing and not treating it as a hobby.

While it is important to record your daily word count to determine how fast you write, you do not need to update your Gantt chart daily. Set appropriate blocks of time for the length of your project. If your book project will take months to complete, you might find tracking your progress on a weekly basis works well. If your timeframe for your book project is one month, then daily updates might help you stay on track better.

NOTE: Your Gantt chart is a handy tool but don't obsess over it

Checking your Gantt Chart too often can cause your Critical Mind to worry more about making progress and less about doing a great job. Keep your Creative Mind away from word counts and target dates. Don't update or check your Gantt Chart more than once at the end of your work day. If you find yourself staring to obsess over your word count, update your Gantt Chart at the end of the week, rather than the end of the day.

Publisher deadlines

If you are offered a traditional publishing contract, the editor will assign a due date for all materials to be submitted. The time to determine whether you can make that deadline is BEFORE you sign the contract.

Your publisher needs a reliable deadline. Chances are, if your proposed deadline is at all close to the original deadline, they will agree to a short delay, as they do not want you to promise to meet a deadline you can't possibly hit.

Before you tell the publisher you cannot meet their deadline, determine how much time you will need by going through the following process:

1) **Determine if you can meet the publisher's deadline.** Identify the tasks you need to complete; the time you guesstimate it will take you to finish those tasks. *If this is your first book, include more time than you think it will take to complete each task.* When building your schedule, start the first task on the date you can actually start working on the project. If you have to complete other projects, and can't start on this one for fourteen days, then don't include those two weeks as project time.

2) **Add extra time to your projections.** If you determine you can finish the project prior to the publisher's deadline, identify these as your extra days. Include the time to your schedule and assign them to the more difficult or time-consuming tasks. See if you can modify your schedule to meet the assigned deadline.

3) **If you calculate that you cannot meet the publisher's deadline,** review your task list and the time you scheduled to complete each task.

4) **Be realistic.** Avoid thinking that you can double or triple your output per day to finish on time. Some people like to think they do best when they get close to the deadline. In reality, this is a very risky strategy putting you one disaster away from missing your deadline.

TIP: Meeting tight deadlines

You can meet a tight deadline by:

1) Writing more hours per day across the duration of the project.
2) Writing at a faster pace.
3) Shorting the length of the book by tightening its focus.

WARNING: Do not cut content to the point where you lower the quality of the book.

Your long-term career will fare better if you turn down a project with a deadline you can't make, than if you accept a project deadline and then have to ask for more time.

Many entrepreneurs fail to understand this lesson, but it remains one of the most important strategies for establishing your reputation as a professional.

If you can't do a good job on a project in the time available, then either negotiate a later deadline or gracefully turn down the job.

You will enjoy more success if you make sure you deliver on time, every time, than if you take on every job and push yourself to your limit only to deliver a sub-par product or miss your deadline, both of which hurt your reputation and your image.

Indie publisher deadlines

Self-publishers and indie publishers take on more responsibilities than simply writing the book. Often the indie publisher's task list includes ordering covers, booking time for copyediting and proofreading, and marketing tasks including pre-launch reviews and platform positioning, etc.

You need to integrate these important, non-writing tasks into your schedule, because you must complete these tasks as part of the book project.

Just like your writing tasks, these tasks must be listed, and time estimates made and added to your chart. Don't double-book yourself. You cannot write and do non-writing tasks at the same time, so give yourself the time you need to complete everything by the deadline.

What to do when you find yourself ahead of your schedule

We would all love to find ourselves blowing our schedule out of the water by writing so fast we finish weeks ahead of where we expected when the deadline arrives.

Don't take a day off even if you feel you have earned it. (You should take sick days. No sense losing a month of writing time when you could have rested, recuperated and gone back to writing.)

If you finish a task early, keep writing.

Put in the hours you originally planned. Get down the word count you set for yourself. You may be ahead now, but the universe has a way of balancing itself out, and that usually means you will need this extra time later in the project.

You can celebrate finishing early the day you actually finish the book.

An example of how to catch up when you get behind - the *Meeting the Writer's Deadline* project

While writing this book, I had an unanticipated family event reduced my productivity for a couple of weeks. I kept writing, but my productivity went down. Finishing a book late that tells everyone else how to meet their own book deadlines would be embarrassing, to say nothing of the damage to my credibility.

I decided to use my experience writing this book as an example of how to catch up. Here are the steps I used to make my deadline:

1) I switched from counting words written per day to concentrating on days available per chapter.
2) I took the number of chapters I had left to write and then divided them by the number of days to finish.
3) I distributed the days between the potential lengths of the chapters. During the process, I realized I could combine two chapters. This eliminated some overlap I hadn't noticed when I wrote the outline.
4) I started writing two hours earlier than normal in the morning, which gave me more hours to write.
5) I cut my lunch break from 1 hour to 30 minutes. (I write full time so this is under my control.)
6) I switched from my usual writing schedule of writing for 25 minutes with a five-minute break to 45 minutes with a fifteen-minute break. This actually gave me 5 minutes more break time, while the longer writing sessions allowed me to work more intensely and keep the pace up longer.

Non-fiction book schedules follow more predictable paths than fiction books. Using the detailed outlines make tracking progress easier for me. Many non-fiction writers develop the ability to estimate the approximate number of words they want for each chapter.

Of course, not every chapter behaves as expected, even for non-fiction authors. Sometimes a chapter goes much longer than expected. Sometimes two chapters merge.

Here, as in fiction writing, trust your Creative Mind. Don't panic. That leads to writer's block. Stay calm and keep writing. If you are like most writers, you will question what you write. Mid-way through a writing project, your Critical Mind often tries to take over. Ignore your doubts and keep writing. When you finish the book you can go back, read what you wrote, and marvel at how well you did! Remember, the Critical Mind likes to boss the Creative Mind around. Don't let it.

The importance of communicating with your team

If you follow the advice in this book, there is a good chance you will finish your book projects on time. You will get better at hitting your deadlines the more you practice, just as you got better at writing with practice.

Armed with what you have learned, you should either complete your book by the deadline or, at a minimum, have a very good idea of how much of a delay you will have before completing your book.

Here is an important rule to follow: Your reputation can handle the occasional missed deadline if you communicate to those who depend on you that you will be delayed, and give them a dependable delivery date.

Surprises are great in thrillers movies and books, but they will ruin your reputation if you miss your deadline and don't let those who are dependent on you know you are going to submit your material late. Your delays cost them money, and that loss gets passed back to you in refusal to work with you or increased fees in anticipation your next job will be submitted later than you promise.

Every writer experiences unavoidable delays at some point. The best planning in the world can't make up for a month-long hospital stay or a fire that destroys the only copy of your book (although, you should have backups of all your files stored off site, so you never lose work in such a manner).

When you realize that you are not going to finish your book on time, revise your time estimates and include extra time. Update your schedule. Calculate your new deadline, contact your publisher and/or production team and explain that you will be delayed in turning in your book. Then ask to move your deadline to your new due date.

Don't procrastinate communicating with your publisher and/or writing team. Delays will be forgiven if people learn about them early enough to adjust on their end.

Top three chapter points to remember

- You can't determine if you will meet your deadline if you don't use some method or tool to tell you how much work you have left to do and if you have time to complete the work.
- There are number of things you can do to catch up when you get behind, but you need to realize you are behind while there is still time to adjust to meet your deadline.
- If you realize you can't meet your deadline, tell everyone who is connected with the project you will need more time and give an honest estimate of how much time you will need.

Chapter 6: Stage 4 – Monitoring Your Budget

In addition to tracking your time, you also want your book project to be completed without exceeding your book budget. Just twenty years ago, a book budget consisted of:

- Research expenses (books, copying costs, etc.)
- Travel expenses
- The value of your time
- Cost of typewriter ribbon
- Cost of paper
- Cost of stamps to mail the completed manuscript to an agent

Thanks to the internet, many of these costs have gone down. However, we now have additional costs that can potentially drive our book budgets up so they exceed earlier financial requirements.

Types of costs associated with a traditional publishing project

Authors who write for traditional publishers enjoy lower costs than indie publishers because they avoid the costs of producing their books. On the other hand, they receive 15% of the profits rather than 70%, so this trade-off does not always mean their company receives a financial benefit.

Typical costs for those writing for a traditional publisher include:

- Research expenses (books, copying costs, etc.)
- Travel expenses
- The value of your time

Your internet service, application monthly fees, etc., are sunk costs – costs you would pay no matter how many books you write – and therefore are counted as separate from the cost of writing a specific book.

An example of a sunk cost would be purchasing a copy of MS Word. Once you buy the program, you can write numerous books without additional costs.

TIP: Know your tax deductions!

The cost of computers, software, subscriptions services, marketing apps, advertising, etc. can be deducted from your taxes! If you are not familiar with the deductions you can get for your writing business, call up an accountant familiar with deductions for authors! You want to take advantage of those deductions.

Types of costs associated with an indie publishing project

As indicated earlier, in this book I use the term "indie-publisher" to refer to an author who outsources most, if not all, of the production aspects of creating a book.

The budget item list for an indie publisher is much longer than for a traditionally published author. Fear of this long to-do list scares many authors from trying to indie publish their work. To be honest, this fear kept me from indie publishing for several years, but during that time a lot of traditional publishers laid-off many of their professional editors, cover designers, and interior book designers and marketing staff. Programmers created tools that made producing and selling books much easier. (See Chapter 8 for a list of recommended tools.)

Book projects for indie authors can include the following expenses: (Customize this list for your typical expenses. Every writer's list is different depending on their business goals, objectives and their budget.)

- Research expenses (books, eBooks, etc.)
- Travel expenses
- The value of your time
- The value of your co-author's time
- Cover designer
- Copyeditor
- Proofreader
- Interior design, if required
- ISBN number
- Bar Code number
- Intellectual lawyer fee,(if a contract is involved and must be reviewed)
- Advertising expenses
- Book website designer/maintenance
- Plug-in renewal fees
- Book domain name
- Marketing/analytic application costs
- Insurance for your publishing company
- Miscellaneous costs

Depending on how much of the production work you do, you may not have all of these expenses. You should make a list, though, and take care not to exceed your budget, as these costs can escalate quickly. Follow M.L. Buchman's advice: ask yourself if an expenditure helps you save a buck or make a buck!

The value of your time

The Writer's Business Plan introduced the idea of the value of the writer's time. There are many things you can do with your time. Most authors would write whether or not they received money for their work. However, when you run a writing business, you should get paid for your time. One way to track this is to track the hours you write and assign a value to that time.

A reasonable way to calculate the value of your time is to use the rate you earned at your last job you worked where you were paid on a per hour basis. You can calculate the cost of your time for writing your book by multiplying the hours you worked by the value of your time. If you take 240 hours to write your book, and the value of your time is $50 hour then the cost of your labor to create the book equals $12,000. If the value of your time is $20/hour then the cost of your labor to create the book equals $4,800. Over time, you want to increase the value of your time!

Most writing businesses do not earn more money than they spend for the first three years. However, when your writing business starts producing a comfortable margin of revenue (you will have to determine how much you define as "comfortable"), you want to begin to take money out of the business.

Your business cannot be described as viable, unless you can take a salary without bankrupting your company. Try to have a plan to do this in five years or less.

Setting your budget

Budget estimates are made during the preparation stage of the book project. Estimate the costs based on prior experience. If you have no prior experience, guess! You will get better at predicting your costs as you launch more books.

TIP: Include budget estimating in your Stage 2 Tasks

Don't forget to include the time to estimate and get quotes on your budget items when calculating the time required for your book project! If you are writing a series, you will find that your original time estimates for establishing your budget tend to be pretty consistent from book to book in a series.

As the project progresses, keep a spreadsheet of incoming revenue from sales coming from online retailers such as Kobo, Amazon, iBooks, etc. or advances received from your traditional publishers.

Also, track your outgoing costs. You can create a spreadsheet to track this information. Many banks now offer online access to your bank account and will generate reports that track this for you.

Another way to collect this information is through an online program like Online QuickBooks. If you know or learn to do simple math in Excel, you can create of modify a simple spreadsheet to track this information yourself.

In your spreadsheet, differentiate between committed costs you must undertake, and costs you plan to do, but can eliminate if confronted by an unforeseen cost.

By tracking your budget throughout the project, you will have time to adjust if your expenses rise too high. Don't despair if you get behind on logging your expenses. Everyone finds themselves in this situation from time to time. Establish a catch-up day once a month for all administrative work. Some authors like to designate a non-writing day for updating their financial spreadsheet with incoming revenues and outgoing expenses.

Form the habit of regularly reviewing your financial situation. Just don't get so focused on your revenue and cash coming in and going out that your writing suffers! The money will stop coming in if you aren't creating books to sell! (I have heard stories of authors that spent so much time tracking their Amazon sales reports that they got behind on their book project!)

Tracking your budget

The best way to prevent going over budget is to agree on the costs with sub-contractors associated with the project before you start writing, and to avoid making changes once you have accepted quotes for producing your book. If you are not confident you can meet a deadline, wait until after your book is written before hiring a sub-contractor. You may have to wait a bit longer if they are busy, but you won't have to worry about missing your deadline and having to postpone the delivery date. Changes to the due date after your subcontractor commits to doing your project often results in penalty or overtime costs. To avoid this situation, follow these guidelines:

Make a list of all costs associated with writing your book. Expenses for a typical fiction book would include:

- Book Cover Creation
- eBook and print
- Copyediting
- Proofreading
- Interior Design or Book Formatting Software (eBook and Print)
- Audio version of book
- Launch Plan
- Advertising budget, if any
- Giveaway's, such as Bookmarks
- Appearance costs, including travel, meals, etc.
- Add a buffer in case some costs go up – such as if your proofreader gets sick and you have to hire someone else at the last moment.
- Enter these costs on a simple spreadsheet:

An Example Of A Production Budget

Production Task List	Budget	Actual Costs	Under/(Over)
Book cover creation			
Ebook	$50.00	$75.00	-$25.00
Print book	$50.00	$30.00	$20.00
Copyeditor	$750.00	$750.00	$0.00
Proofreader	$250.00	$250.00	$0.00
Interior designer			
Ebook	$250.00	$250.00	$0.00
Print book	$250.00	$250.00	$0.00
Audio version of book	$750.00	$750.00	$0.00
Advertising	$150.00	$135.00	$15.00
Graphics/banners for website	$50.00	$40.00	$10.00
Giveaways			
Bookmarks	$35.00	$35.00	$0.00
Video	$800.00	$800.00	$0.00
Appearances			
Travel	$500.00	$200.00	$300.00
Meals	$200.00	$100.00	$100.00
Total Budget	$4,085.00	$3,665.00	$420.00

Under Total Budget, you can see that this project came in $420 under the original estimate.

When you exceed your budget

You need a plan for what to do if your costs exceed your planned budget. One easy way to go over-budget is to make an unexpected purchase. Have a checklist for determining if you should go through with the purchase, and how you will adjust your budget so you don't put your company at financial risk of failure if you make the purchase.

Check list for determining if you should make an unforeseen purchase:

- ❑ What benefit does the purchase provide for the business?
- ❑ Is there a way to accomplish the same result for free?
- ❑ Is there a way to accomplish the same result for less money?
- ❑ What about the purchase makes it much better than the free or less expensive alternative?
- ❑ Does the benefit described above help you achieve more revenue faster than the free or less-expensive alternative?
- ❑ How much additional revenue does the purchase provide than the free or less-expensive alternatives?
- ❑ Does the purchase save you time that would allow you to produce more books faster?
- ❑ Does the purchase replace an existing service(s) you use?
- ❑ Is the purchase less expensive than the service you are replacing?
- ❑ Is the purchase in your business plan in the future, and does a discount or special pricing save you money over the long run?

Did I leave something out? Just add any additional questions to make a checklist tailored to you! You can download this Checklist at:

www.BusinessBooksForWriters/MTWD_Budget_Checklist

Once you complete the checklist and determine that it makes business sense to make the purchase (i.e. the purchase will make your money faster or will save you more money than the service costs), then you need to adjust your budget so that you stay within budget while making the purchase.

How to adjust your budget for an unexpected purchase

Budgets get thrown off all the time, and often for good reason. What do you do if a new online marketing service that you've wanted for a long time is now available at 50% off for a week? With this app, you're expect to increase your sales by 30% per month. If you sign up for a yearly payment of $400 for the new app, you can eliminate an app you are already using that costs $250 per year.

You feel, based on your business plan, that taking advantage of this offer would be a smart business move. However, signing up for the app will push your expenses over your anticipated monthly budget.

When facing a tight company budget, you have several options:

1) Pass on the purchase. Yes, the new service could increase your revenues, but the program will still be available in a year. Most companies offer discount sales at least one time a year, so while you may pay a bit more for the service at the next sale, in the meantime, your company can continue to pay the bills.

2) Eliminate a planned expenditure or two in your company budget that costs as much as the service you want to get, but will not produce equal revenues. If you can't find any expenses to cut, then don't be afraid to pass on the new program and stick with your plan of purchasing it next year when you have a larger budget.
3) Don't be afraid to forego an expenditure if you do not have enough money to make the purchase. Stay within a comfortable budget. You will sleep better at night.

Top three chapter points to remember

- Just as you need to track your progress toward finishing your book project, you also need to track your expenditures and the money you are making through your online sales or advances from your publisher.
- Indie publishers should make a list of what was bought to produce the book. Only count what you paid for to produce the book.
- Software, office expenses, etc. might count for tax deductions. Get an accountant familiar with IRS and your state's deductions for authors as they vary from state to state.

Chapter 7: Stage 5- Closing Your Book Project

You finished before your deadline, but you are not done

If you follow the advice in this book, you will greatly increase the probability of completing your book project before your deadline. Congratulations! But don't celebrate yet.

I know writing a book requires a great deal of mental and physical effort, and leaves most writers exhausted. However, before you move on to the next great book idea that has taken over every waking minute of your life, you should close out the current project by updating your records and recording what you learned from the experience.

This extra effort will help you become a more efficient writer, improve your ability to meet your future deadlines, and ensure your heirs benefit from your work.

File your documents

When you finish your book, take the time to archive your files, saving them to a folder where you can find them. Then review them when you get ready to start on your next project.

Here are the documents you want to archive:

- Your task estimates
- Your Gantt chart
- Your daily word count
- Your project budget
- The electronic files for all versions of your book (eBook, print, audio)
- The jpgs or electronic files of the book cover
- Electronic promotional files (bookmarks, etc.)

As part of your filing, take a moment to review each document and write down changes you want to make in your approach for the next book.

Review your process flowcharts and delete unnecessary steps and/or add steps that would have made the process easier, simpler, or faster for you. Save time by referring to these documents when you sit down to set a realistic deadline for your next book. Author Carlos Valcarcel recommends you create templates from your last files to use for the next project. Include actions you want to replicate in the template.[16]

Your books are assets

Every book you complete becomes a company asset. If you don't have a list of all your assets, start one. This is important both for insurance purposes, and for your heirs. You should also update your business plan's financial projection actuals for your future reference.

Looking out for your heirs

The intellectual property rights for your book continue for 70 years after your death. When your book is finished, you want to file all the information related to the book project and inform your heirs of the location of this information. You will save them a lot of time when they have to access these documents as part of your estate.

Unless your heirs work for your company, they probably don't understand your business or the value of your intellectual property. If you are not familiar with a writer's letter to the heirs, check out this summary of a very good blog post written by JA Konrath, entitled "Death and the Self-Pubbed Writer."[17] The post identifies why writers need to leave a letter for heirs, and the information that should be included. In brief, you want to make sure that your heirs have a list of all your company's assets, what rights you have retained for each asset, any rights you have licensed, dates your rights revert back to you, etc.

Here is another good article you will want to read by the lawyer who writes online as Passive Guy, "What Happens

When an Author Dies?".[18] You will find some great information here about U.S. inheritance taxes, trusts, etc. Read the comments too, as they contain information of interest as well. (If you're an author in a country other than the United States, you'll want to research the details specific to your country.)

If you have no heirs, then you might consider leaving the intellectual property rights to your writing to your alma mater. Universities have the knowledge, space, and expertise to look after your rights, after your death. Do be sure to contact the university ahead of time to see what requirements must be met, and to ensure you approve of how they would to handle your writings.

Lessons learned

After you have completed your book and sent it off to either your copy editor or traditional editor, take the time to write up what you did well and what you could improve or would change.

Pull up this "lessons learned" document after you have finished the ideas stage of your next book. These lessons will serve to remind you of the approach you want to meet future projects' deadlines, and will lead to new ways to further improve your process. In addition, reviewing your word counts will show you the improvements you made in your writing pace.

A lessons learned example

In *The Writer's Business Plan,* I talked about how you write a business plan and then update it as you gain experience and learn more about the publishing business. This helps your plan improve over time, and turns what could quickly become an old document into a dynamic tool that records your increasing knowledge, ideas, and strategies for building your business.

You want to continuously improve your ability to meet your book deadlines as well. Over time, you want to become very good at knowing how fast you write – and you want to learn to write faster, because the more predictable your writing pace (the number of words you write per hour/day, or however you decide to track your speed), the better you will become at predicting the time required to write your next book.

Many authors don't record when they start their writing day and when they stop. I didn't do this for years, and when I started, I couldn't believe how many fewer hours I wrote than what I thought. This meant I actually wrote faster than I believed, because my word count accrued in much less time that I estimated.

Writing down my word count reassures me that, in fact, I can make my deadlines. Documenting my mistakes and listing new ideas I came up with an increasing writing efficiency without sacrificing creativity, which helps me improve my ability to meet my future book project deadlines.

Work hard, but work smart – the value of taking care of yourself

You write best when you are physically healthy. A key part of being able to meet your deadline requires you to take care of yourself. You need to make time for your physical and mental well-being when you design your schedule.

When you get behind on your schedule, or when you are juggling a writing career with a family and a full time job, you may find yourself thinking you just need to cut out all activities and spend your available time writing. You think if you spend longer hours at the keyboard you will catch up, but a serious danger lurks in this line of reasoning.

You can push yourself for a few days, but prolonged stretches of forcing yourself to work like this can backfire. If you are a full time writer, falling into a lifestyle of working, eating, sleeping, and writing at the expense of the rest of the rest of your life can harm your writing career, your company's success and on your relationship with your family.

When you are pushing hard to make a deadline, you need to teach yourself to recognize when you need a break. Here are some classic signs you are working your brain too hard:

- You start daydreaming of things besides the chapter you are writing.

- You leave the writing to read email or catch up on Facebook or play video games or watch TV. Be honest with yourself. Take a break, set a timer, and when the timer goes off, go back to work.
- You get sleepy in the middle of the day.
- You are physically tired.
- You get irritable.
- You become forgetful.
- You become angry all the time.

If you want to stick to your schedule, you need to be purposeful in how you use your time. Make a plan and stick with it. Get seven to eight hours of sleep. Do this even if your eight hours are from 2 am until 10 am.

Find time for exercise. It is easy to put off exercise, but it is important, even if you only exercise for fifteen minutes a day. In the book, *Manage Your Day-to-Day: Build Your Routine, Find Your Focus, and Sharpen Your Creative Mind (The 99U Book Series),*[19] Scott McDowell writes in his essay, "Training Your Mind To Be Ready For Insight," many of "our brightest minds have used some combination of daily spiritual or physical preparation. He quotes a Newsweek article that states, "Exercise sharpens brain activity. Almost every dimension of cognition improves from thirty minutes of aerobic exercise, and creativity is no exception. The type of exercise doesn't matter, and the boost lasts for at least two hours afterward."[20]

Another great article to read is "The Creative Brain on Exercise." This article by Jonathan Fields in Fast Company discusses the many benefits writers get from exercise.[21]

In addition to exercise, include time for your family. Being a successful entrepreneur doesn't mean you have to sacrifice your family life despite common assumptions.

Many writers find that writing takes so much energy and concentration, that they can only write for four hours a day. At 500 words an hour, that is still 2000 words a day. At this rate, your 60,000-word novel will take 30 working days to complete. You still finish in a month.

When you work up your schedule, include a half hour for exercise, and a half hour each for breakfast and lunch, and an hour for dinner. So far, you've used between four and eight hours of your day. You have plenty of time for the rest of your life.

If you skip eating well or don't exercise, your health could decline. You might start to lack the energy to sit for four to eight hours a day. Your productivity will decline. Ideas often start to take longer to come. You might find it hard to even write 500 words an hour. Lack of sleep often leads to higher stress. You might lose sleep. None of this helps your writing.

Burnout remains one of the dangers for writers facing a never-ending stream of tight deadlines. This is especially a concern for self-publishers and indie publishers who have so many different tasks to do. Make sure you understand how to recognize burnout, and how to avoid getting yourself into this dangerous health situation. Burnout is **NOT** a badge of honor of the dedicated writer; it is a serious health hazard of our profession. To learn more about how to recognize and avoid burnout, read these articles:

- "10 signs that you have a case of writing burnout" by Andi Marquette[22]
- "Recover from Writing Burn Out: 18 Tips for Writing with Gusto" by Tess Marshall[23]
- *5 Ways to Recover After a Writing Burnout* – a guest teaching session with Nichole Severn[24]

You do not want to go through severe burnout. Remember, it is better to avoid burnout by establishing a routine that prevents it, than to have to recover from burnout. If you want a long writing career without interruption, follow the advice in these articles and keep yourself from burning out.

Top three chapter points to remember

- Take the time after you finish writing to set yourself up for future success by documenting what went well during your book project and what you do not want to repeat. After a few years of accumulating these "lessons learned", you will find you have made considerable progress in meeting your deadlines.
- Keep a file of your published and unpublished work and document where the files are located. Tell your heirs where the files are stored. The intellectual property rights for your book will continue for 70 years after your death. Your heirs will thank you for your foresight.

- One of the best things you can do for yourself is look after your health so you can keep writing. Get eight hours of sleep, follow a healthy lifestyle and avoid working non-stop. Avoid burnout. It is a very quick way to end your writing career.

Chapter 8: Tools To Help You Meet Your Deadlines

Several years ago I wrote, but didn't try to market, a number of novels. I wanted to see how the publishing industry would evolve. I had many choices. Should I market my fiction to a traditional publishing house through an agent? Should I send my manuscripts direct to an acquisition editor? Should I self-publish?

Self-publishing made little sense to the business side of my personality. I had successfully launched two profitable companies, and I couldn't imagine trying to do all of the publishing tasks myself. So I kept writing, and let my manuscripts sit on my computer's hard drive.

Then the publishing industry finally matured to the point I could plan my strategy. The consolidation of traditional publishers meant that a lot of knowledgeable copy editors, interior book designers, and cover artists had began to freelance. I could subcontract this work to professionals who would do a far better job.

After gathering recommendations from other writers and hiring a number of people to do small projects, I chose the best graphic designer, copyeditor, and interior book designer from among the subcontractors I had used.

Then I launched Magnolia Lane Press.

The marketing and business strategy I could do myself. These activities take time, but a business owner knows what they want to do with their company better than anyone else.

You know how you want people to think of your company. You know how much time and effort you want to put into your company. You know how much money you have to invest in your company.

Hopefully, you sat down and wrote up your company business plan so that you (and your heirs, if they inherit the company), know your goals for your publishing business and the strategies you plan to pursue to accomplish those goals.

During my four-year period before starting an indie publishing company, another very important development occurred: a number of great productivity and marketing tools sprang up that allowed writers to write faster and manage the business side of their company much more efficiently.

New tools appear every day. As soon as a blogger publishes a list of tools to use, a new tools list emerges. To help keep the information in this book current, the Business Books For Writer's "Resource" page contains an updated list of the tools I have tried and recommend as well as tools readers have suggested:

www.businessbooksforwriters.com/resources

While the most favored tool may change from year to year or week to week, the existing tool developers keep up by releasing new updates. For this reason, it often isn't worth changing tools every time a new one hits the market.

Here are number of tools you may find helpful in keeping your book project under control.

Tools and apps for tracking your time

Pacemaker - Web-based service

We discussed the use of a Gantt chart to show how a writer can calculate the time required to complete their book and the advantages of including extra time in a book project plan.

An alternative to a Gantt chart that many writers might find less intimidating would be a program such as **Pacemaker**, www.pacemaker.press. This free, web-based program offers some nice features. You can estimate your word count for a single project, or simply set a number of words you want to write over a period of time. You can write the same amount of words per day or weight certain days. You can set some dates as non-writing days.

Based on your actual word count, the program calculates how many words you need to write to "catch up" to your desired total, if you lag behind. You can also set up your schedule so you write the bulk of your words at the start of the project, to ensure you have less to write at the end of the project! To help you get started you can base your plan on a sample plan.

For a free program, you get a lot of nice features.

Chrono plus (Mac OS only, but if there are iPhone and iPad versions)

I track my writing time using two programs. First, I use **Chrono Plus** to track the actual time I am writing. Many consultants use Chrono Plus to track the time they spend on a specific client's work. There is an option to set an hourly rate. I use this tool, because it reminds me that my time is valuable – and it reminds me of the true cost of the book I have written. One other feature I like is that you can set the amount of idle time before the program asks you if you want to count the idle time or not.

This comes in handy when you encounter an unavoidable interruption, and it increases the accuracy of time log.

You can generate reports from Chrono Plus. I don't use this feature much. Instead, I usually log the time on my writing spreadsheet.

Chrono Plus also allows you to set up multiple projects and track the cost of your time. You can enter the value of your time (i.e. your hourly wage). The program tracks the time you work on each task. Sum the time spent writing and multiply by the value of your time. If you feel a fair wage for your writing time is $20/hour and you spend 30 days times six hours a day writing (180 hours), the value of labor writing the book is equal to $3,500 (180*20). This exercise inspires me to avoid wasting time and keeps me from procrastinating because the sooner I finish the current book, the sooner I can start the next book and make more money. I still want to write the best book I can, I just understand that wasted time, (not time spent contemplating or imagining, but truly wasted time, works against my success as an author.)

PC Chrono

I haven't found a great PC equivalent to Chrono Plus but check out **PC Chrono**, www.highspheres.com/products/pc_chrono, as a decent alternative for PC users. If you have a PC timer that you love please let me know at TPrice@TonyaPrice.com. I would love to add it to the Business Books For Writers resource page.

Toggl - (Mac OS, Windows, Android and iOS)

Toggl, www.toggl.com, offers a free account, as well as various pricing choices.

If you are not already using a timer and tracking program, then you might want to consider Toggl. This program comes with Timer, a nice dashboard and reports. With the paid version, you can have the program automatically track a fee per hour. Unlike Chrono Plus, this is not included in the free version.

The paid version of Toggl includes summary, detailed, and weekly reports. You can also create teams, which could come in handy if you have a co-author and want to coordinate your work or see how much they are accomplishing! There is also a mobile app.

Pomodoro Timers

I discovered the **Pomodoro** timer method while writing *The Writer's Business Plan*. The book had a very short deadline, and I had to work long hours. I would focus so hard on the writing that I would forget to eat and take breaks. I came very close to burning myself out.

As a former computer programmer, I had experienced issues with carpal tunnel syndrome before, and knew if I went through that again, I would not be able to write for an extended period of time.

Luckily, I read an article on the Lifehacker.com website about the Pomodoro technique, "Productivity 101: A Primer to The Pomodoro Technique."[25]

You can buy books on the origins and concepts behind Pomodoro, but basically, followers divide their work schedule into 25-minute work periods, separated by either 5-minute or 15-minute breaks. Most people can work for 25 minutes at a time. If you are tempted to stop and check email or surf the web, the Pomodoro technique lets you know you have to just keep working for a bit more before you are going to have a break. This reduces the temptation to arbitrarily take breaks that quickly escalate into hours rather than minutes– or when you forget to go back to the computer to start your next 25-minute period!

Look for a timer that lets you adjust the length of

individual time segments. When you get behind, you can set your timer to a longer work period followed by a shorter break if you decide you would rather go for longer stretches between rest periods.

Be Focused Pro - (Mac OS)

I prefer Pomodoro times that let me adjust the time between breaks and the length of the breaks. There is also a free version of Be Focused with fewer customization options. Get this first to see if you benefit from this approach. http://apple.co/2mNSyYd

FocusBooster - (Mac OS, Windows).

Focus Booster offers many of the same Pomodoro features of Be Focused Pro. You can start with a free account and upgrade if you wish to a monthly or yearly plans. www.focusboosterapp.com

Additional ways to avoid distractions

If you find it hard to avoid the temptation to work on everything but your writing, how do you focus on your manuscript?

First, you can work in short bursts and tell yourself that if you work until your scheduled break time, you can then make a phone call, check your email, catch up on Facebook posts, etc. As mentioned above a writing/break schedule such as advocated by the Pomodoro technique encourages you to keep moving forward.

Many writers turn off their phones during their writing time, or at least turn off the ringers.

You can also turn off your Wi-Fi connection to avoid the temptation of web surfing and email checking! Go ahead – try it!

On a Mac:

1) Finding the four stacked curved lines at the top right of your screen.
2) Click on the Wi-Fi icon, and then
3) Click on "Turn Wi-Fi Off."
4) On a PC with Windows 10:
5) Step 1: Click on "windows" icon
6) Step 2: Click on gear icon for settings
7) Step 3: Click on "Network and Internet"
8) Step 3: Slide Wi-Fi to "Off"
9) You can turn Wi-Fi on when you want Wi-Fi active again.

If you're having trouble, the "Dummies" their website has a good article, *How to Disable Wi-Fi Access on Your Windows Laptop,* www.dummies.com. You can read about how to turn off wireless for various PC laptops.

When you turn your Wi-Fi connection off, you won't need to worry about notifications popping up, email notices, etc. And you can turn it back on at the end of your writing day.

As I mentioned earlier, some writers reduce Internet temptations by having two computers and sometimes even two offices. When they are writing, they work at desk, they use *only for writing* and a computer that does not have internet access. Temptation is easier to keep out when you don't let it in!

Depending on your self-discipline, you can avoid temptation by using the "Focus View" Option in your word processing program.

The focus view icon for Scrivener is the blue box with a two-ended diagonal arrow. Click on this, and all you see on your computer screen is your writing page on a black background. (If you are unfamiliar with Scrivener, see the tip box below for information on this writer's tool.)

Microsoft Word offers a similar option. On an Apple Mac, the focus icon is the last icon on the bottom left of the writing page and looks like a black rectangle with a camera-like viewfinder. Click on this icon, and you will see just your writing page on a black background. Hit the Escape key, and either program will take you back to the normal view.

NOTE: A word about Scrivener

Many writers use **Scrivener**. If you are unfamiliar with Scrivener, it is described by the company as "a complete writing studio". Many writers write their manuscripts in

Scrivener. You can export your manuscript as an epub or mobi file for uploading your eBook to an online retailer. This does not work well for non-fiction books with tables and bullet points.

I recommend hiring an internal book designer for non-fiction books. It will save you money and hours of frustration. I use Dean Fetzer of GunBoss Books, www.gunboss.com, as the interior book designer for the *Business Books For Writers* series and he is fantastic.

I use Scrivener to organize all my book projects. You can store your research, including links to web pages, jpgs, and documents like contracts in Scrivener. This makes locating information easy.

I do want to provide a warning though – there is a learning curve when you start out with Scrivener. If you are interested in the product, investigate Gwen Hernandez' course, **Scrivener 101**, www.scrivenerclasses.com. I took the course and it is worth every penny.

Top three chapter points to remember

- There are very talented people available to help you form a team if you decide to indie publish your work. A reliable team allows you to spend more time writing.

- There are many tools available to help you be more productive. Don't be afraid to try new tools, but don't spend all your time learning new tools either. Once you find a good tool, stay with it.
- Scrivener is a program developed for writers by writers. If you are unfamiliar with this program, check it out and if it looks useful, consider taking Gwen Hernandez' course.

Chapter 9: A Final Word

Every writer has a different reason for writing. Most of us start out because we can't not write.

Then we start to show our friends our writing and they encourage us because they love our stories. So we write some more and at some point where we decide to try to sell our writing.

Now that there are so many tools available, we artists cannot only create our books but we can produce them, distribute them and actually make enough money to grow a viable business from our work. Some writers write but never show their stories to anyone.

A great many writers write and try to sell to others for validation that they are a good writer.

A few writers write and want to make enough money from their writing so they can write full time and quit their day job.

All of these approaches are valid. Decide the kind of writer you want to be and if you want to be a writing entrepreneur, who makes money to not only survive but also thrive, then remember:

1) When you establish a reputation as a writer who meets deadlines more opportunities will come your way.
2) Every goal needs a deadline.
3) To meet a deadline you need to write down your deadline, commit to meeting that deadline, track and write down your progress.
4) When you have met your deadline, take M.L. Buchman's advice: CELEBRATE your success!

Remember:

There is no single way to meet a deadline. There is no single tool. This book has presented ideas for you to try so you can find which approaches and tools best fit the way you work.

Don't be afraid to experiment with different approaches.

Don't be afraid to try new tools.

Don't be afraid to alter your approach. In fact, expect it. In business, nothing stays the same year after year. That is the fun part of being a writing entrepreneur!

Additional Resources

I included a number of resources in *The Writer's Business Plan* to help you continue to improve your business plan and to give you more ideas about how to succeed in your writing career. Like publishing, information on the Web changes frequently. The *Resources* page on the *Business Books for Writers* website

www.businessbooksforwriters.com/resources

contains updates for links contained in any of the books in the series, as well as new resources of interest to readers.

Do you have a resource you would recommend to be added to the Resources page? Send your recommendation to Webmaster@BusinessBooksForWriters.com, and the information will be added to the list so other writers (including me), can see and benefit from your suggestion(s).

A Word From The Author

Thank you for purchasing *Meeting the Writer's Deadline*. Please let me know your story of how this book helped you meet your latest book deadline.

I especially want to thank those of you who bought *The Writer's Business Plan* and have now purchased *Meeting the Writer's Deadline*. Your loyalty, emails, and support mean a great deal to me as I develop the *Business Books For Writers* series.

If you find the *Business Books for Writers* valuable, I would appreciate it if you let other writers know about the book at your writing groups and among your network of authors. Word of mouth is the best advertising. Reviews of the book also help spread the word to other authors that there is a resource to help them avoid distractions, manage their time, and start finishing their books on time too.

Your comments on the book will help make future *Business Books For Writers* even better, and your feedback will be incorporated into future updated editions of the book. Please send any comments, questions and suggestions to **TPrice@TonyaPrice.com.** You can also reach me via Twitter: @BusBooks4Writer where I post daily tips and links to articles of interest to writing entrepreneurs on LinkedIn at: www.linkedin.com/in/tonyadprice.

If you would like to continue to get helpful information, business advice, and information on contests, giveaways, and requests to participate in our beta reader program, please sign up for *The Writing Entrepreneur* newsletter at:

www.BusinessBooksForWriters.com/TheWritingEntrepreneur

The Business Books For Writers Series

Authors must juggle many tasks, and while learning boosts success, this series shares important business concepts authors can learn in a weekend. That is why none of the books in the *Business Books For Writers* series exceed 25,000 words.

You will find a great many general business books for writers. Some excellent books tell you everything you want to know about the business side of writing. Some books show you how to self-publish your books in great detail. Some books reveal how to market your books.

The *Business Books For Writers* series focuses on teaching business skills that often prevent writers from implementing the lessons other books teach. If you can't finish your book on time, then you won't be able to implement what you learn in the marketing books your read. If you can't manage your to-do list, you won't have the time to go on book tours and speak at conferences and still have the time to write and publish books.

Book one of the *Business Books For Writers* series, *The Writer's Business Plan*, helps writers develop a business plan for their career, whether their goal was to publish their books themselves or sell their books to traditional publishers. By defining their mission and vision statements and developing a marketing, financial, and strategic plan for their career, writers learned how to set and achieve success over their career.

Book Two, *Meeting the Writer's Deadline,* shows writers how to manage their time to meet their writing deadlines and stay within their budget. The book shares simple ways to control a writing schedule, rather than have a task list control the writer's time. Once authors find themselves in control of their time and free from the stress and worry of missing their deadlines, they often find their creativity escalates and they rediscover the joy of writing again.

Managing an indie publishing company requires great organizational skills, but if you struggle to track expenses, keep your blog up to date, and find time to write, relax! You can *learn* these skills. But you will still miss your deadlines if you don't also develop the habit of *using* these skills. This book provides tips and advice to help you in both these areas.

Book 3, *Completing the Writers To-Do-List,* shows writers how to get things done by managing their to-do list. After the stress of completing your writing by deadline, managing your to-do list is the next biggest stress point you must conquer. The book identifies common obstacles to completing your to-do list items and how to overcome them. You can't do what you can't remember. Learn strategies for tracking your to-do list items so none of them get dropped. Finally, conquer the biggest time sink of all – your email list.

Acknowledgments

I have had a great deal of help on this book from some very talented writers and project managers. My beta readers, Carlos Valcarcel, a fellow Oregon Writers Network member, provided insightful recommendations with just the right sense of humor to make a revision fun! Robert Oakes, Jr., a long time friend and a fantastic Project Management Consultant, zeroed in on how to clarify any project management explanations to ensure accuracy. I am indebted to them for the time and feedback they provided.

I had the great opportunity of interviewing three writers with considerable project management experience. M.L. Buchman, the Romantic Suspense author, Johanna Rothman, author of numerous project management and agile project management books and also a Romance novelist and Ron Collins, indie publisher, Science Fiction author and very experienced project manager. They provided a many practical recommendations and examples that have been incorporated into the book.

Since the early 2000, I have been taking courses with Dean Wesley Smith and Kristine Kathryn Rusch. They are not only award winning authors, and owners of WMG Publishing Inc., but their desire to help writers and their generosity in doing so inspired me to try to give forward by writing a series of books to help writers learn practical business techniques for writing entrepreneurs.

I have had three important mentors throughout my career. The first was Michael Brown, who was my manager and mentor at Hewlett-Packard, where I started my management career. He taught me that a manager's primary role is to help the people who report to them succeed in their careers. I have come to see that this approach is the difference between a manager and a leader.

My second mentor was Geoff Schultz, founder of UltraNet Communications, whose encouragement to go out on my own and found StrategicIdeas.com opened the door for me to launch my first company. Geoff's willingness to bring me back after the company grew so fast that I risked losing everything, allowed me to pull success from failure.

And finally, I owe a great deal of thanks to Thomas Lynch III, CIO at Suffolk University and President of startiTup!, LLC, whose faith in me and whose advice and instruction allowed me to grow as a manager and as a person in ways I never imagined. I will always be indebted to Tom for his support when I made the decision to leave Suffolk University to pursue my dream of launching Magnolia Lane Press. Suffolk is so lucky to have such an outstanding CIO and a true leader.

Through my entire career, I have enjoyed the love, support, and unwavering encouragement from the love of my life, Dr. Kent Albert Jones. Without Kent, I would never have had the success I've known, the stability that allowed me to pursue my dreams, or my wonderful daughters, Ana-Lisa and Diantha, who are my proudest legacy.

Tonya D. Price – Author of *Business Books For Writers*

After thirty years of setting up businesses, both helping others and successfully undertaking two business ventures of my own, I wanted to give back to the writing community. I started writing non-fiction business books for writers, in addition to my fiction writing.

I first became interested in project management at Cornell University while completing my MBA in Marketing and Finance. In 2005,I became certified as a Project Management Professional (PMP) by the Project Management Institute, and remained certified for five years.

I used my knowledge of project management to manage small website projects, as well as oversee the complete redesign of a 40,000-page website at Worcester Polytechnic

Institute. I also spent two years at Suffolk University in Boston, Massachusetts, as Director of the Project Management Office, where I oversaw backend web projects, a Workday Human Capital Management (HCM) and Benefits project, as well as many other IT projects.

In *Meeting the Writer's Deadline,* I draw on my experience managing projects to help writers understand how to manage the creation of their book projects so their books are finished on time and within budget. I considered my knowledge of how to manage writing projects as my greatest asset when I started Magnolia Lane Press and I am excited to be able to share my knowledge with fellow writers. I hope this book helps you achieve your business goals.

Ways to reach Tonya

Email:	TPrice@TonyaPrice.com
Twitter:	@BusBooks4Writers
LinkedIn:	www.linkedin.com/in/tonyadprice/
Facebook:	www.facebook.com/BusinessBooksForWriters
Website:	www.BusinessBooksForWriters.com
Author site:	www.TonyaDPrice.com

Notes

Want easy access to the online links while reading? Go to

www.BusinessBooksForWriters.com/mtwd-links

[1] Gail Matthews, Goals Research Summary, Dominican University, 2015 www.dominican.edu/academics/ahss/undergraduate-programs/psych/faculty/assets-gail-matthews/researchsummary2.pdf.

[2] M.L. Buchman and M.L. Buchman, *Managing Your Inner Artist/Writer: Strategies for Success*, Buchman Bookworks, Inc., 2014.

[3] *A Guide to the Project Management body of Knowledge (PMBOK® Guide)* 5th ed., Project Management Institute, 2013.

[4] Buchman and Buchman.

[5] Matthews.

[6] Roger Parker, "Finishing your book on time and avoiding writers block", Activegarage.com, January 23, 2013, http://bit.ly/2kq5Ni4.

[7] Stephen King, *On Writing – A Memoir of the Craft,* Scribner, 2010.

[8] Michael Pollack, "12 Tips on How to Become a Faster Writer", www.michaeldpollock.com/overcome-writers-block.

[9] Chris Fox, *5,000 Words Per Hour: Write Faster, Write Smarter: Write Faster, Write Smarter,* Chris Fox Writes LLC, 2015.

[10] Monica Leonelle, *Write Better, Faster: How To Triple Your Writing Speed and Write More Every Day (Growth Hacking For Storytellers #1),* Spaulding House, 2015.

[11] Rachel Aaron, *2k to 10k: Writing Faster, Writing Better, and Writing More of What You Love,* 2012.

[12] Michelle Leonelle, *Dictate Your Book: How To Write Your Book Faster, Better, and Smarter (Growth Hacking For Storytellers #4),* Spaulding House, 2015.

[13] Kevin Gise, *Dictation: Dictate Your Writing – Write Over A Million Words A Year Without Breaking A Sweat,* 2016.

[14] Buchman and Buchman.

[15] Wikipedia, Gantt chart, https://en.wikipedia.org/wiki/Gantt_chart.

[16] Carlos Valcarcel, *Eclipse Kick Start,* Sams Publishing, 2004.

[17] J.A. Konrath, "Death and the Self-Pubbed Writer," 27 November 2013, www.thepassivevoice.com/2013/11/death-and-the-self-pubbed-writer.

[18] Passive Guy, "What Happens When an Author Dies?", 8 September 2011, www.thepassivevoice.com/2011/09/what-happens-when-an-author-dies.

[19] Jocelyn K. Glei, ed., *Manage Your Day-to-Day: Build Your Routine, Find Your Focus, and Sharpen Your Creative Mind (The 99U Book Series),* Amazon Publishing, May 21, 2013, "Training Your Mind To Be Ready For Insight," by Scott McDowell, p.183.

[20]Po Bronson and Ashley Merryman, "The Creativity Crisis," Newsweek, July 10, 2010.

[21] Jonathon Fields, *The Creative Brain On Exercise,* Fast Company, 29 September 2011, www.fastcompany.com/1783263/creative-brain-exercise.

[22] Andi Marquette, "10 signs that you have a case of writing burnout", 20 January 2015, http://bit.ly/2jMOdDf.

[23] Tess Marshall, "Recover from Writing Burn Out: 18 Tips for Writing with Gusto", http://bit.ly/2jMAUTm.

[24] Nichole Severn, "5 Ways To Recover After A Writing Burnout", www.well-storied.com/blog/writing-burnout.

[25] Alan Henry, "Productivity 101: A Primer to The Pomodoro Technique", Lifehacker, 2 July 2014, www.lifehacker.com/productivity-101-a-primer-to-the-pomodoro-technique-1598992730.

Made in the USA
Monee, IL
04 November 2026

67385902R10075